The Sacraments

A Continuing Encounter

with Christ

The Sacraments

A Continuing Encounter with Christ

taken from
The Teaching of Christ: A Catholic Catechism for Adults

Donald Cardinal Wuerl

Ronald Lawler, O.F.M. Cap.
Thomas Comerford Lawler
Kris D. Stubna

Edited by Jem Sullivan, Ph.D.

Our Sunday Visitor Publishing Division
Our Sunday Visitor, Inc.
Huntington, IN 46750

Nihil Obstat
Msgr. Michael Heintz, Ph.D.
Censor Librorum

Imprimatur
✠ Kevin C. Rhoades
Bishop of Fort Wayne-South Bend
October 28, 2010

The *Nihil Obstat* and *Imprimatur* are official declarations that a book is free from doctrinal or moral error. It is not implied that those who have granted the *Nihil Obstat* and *Imprimatur* agree with the contents, opinions, or statements expressed.

Every reasonable effort has been made to determine copyright holders of excerpted materials and to secure permissions as needed. If any copyrighted materials have been inadvertently used in this work without proper credit being given in one form or another, please notify Our Sunday Visitor in writing so that future printings of this work may be corrected accordingly.

Our Sunday Visitor Publishing Division
Our Sunday Visitor, Inc.
200 Noll Plaza
Huntington, IN 46750
1-800-348-2440
bookpermissions@osv.com

ISBN: 978-1-59276-827-1 (Inventory No. T1130)
LCCN: 2010938545
Cover design by Rebecca J. Heaston
Cover image: Shutterstock
Interior design by Sherri L. Hoffman

PRINTED IN THE UNITED STATES OF AMERICA

Acknowledgments

THE SCRIPTURE CITATIONS USED in this work are taken from the *Catholic Edition of the Revised Standard Version of the Bible* (RSV), copyright © 1965 and 1966 by the Division of Christian Education of the National Council of the Churches of Christ in the United States of America. Used by permission. Special permission has been received to use the you-your-yours of the personal pronouns in address to God, and to capitalize personal pronouns referring to God.

English translation of the *Catechism of the Catholic Church* for the United States of America copyright © 1994, 1997, United States Catholic Conference, Inc. — Libreria Editrice Vaticana.

Quotations from the Documents, Decrees, and Declarations of the Second Vatican Council used in this book are from the translation, with some amendments, appearing in *The Documents of Vatican II*, Walter M. Abbott, S.J., General Editor. Reprinted with permission of AMERICA. All rights reserved. © 1966 by America Press, 106 W. 56th St., New York, NY 10019.

Sacramentum Caritatis © 2007 by Libreria Editrice Vaticana. Used with permission.

Excerpts from the English translation of *Rite of Baptism for Children* © 1969, International Committee on English in the Liturgy, Inc. (ICEL); excerpts from the English translation of *Rite of Marriage* © 1969, ICEL; excerpts from the English translation of *The Roman Missal* © 1973, ICEL; excerpts from the English translation of *Rite of Penance* © 1974, ICEL; excerpts from the English translation of *Rite of Confirmation (Second Edition)* © 1975, ICEL; excerpts from the English translation of *The Ordination of Deacons, Priests, and Bishops* © 1975, ICEL; excerpts from the English translation of *Pastoral Care of the Sick: Rites of Anointing and Viaticum* © 1982, ICEL; excerpts from the English translation of *Rite of Christian Initiation of Adults* © 1985, ICEL. All rights reserved.

Contents

CCC   *Catechism of the Catholic Church*
GS   *Gaudium et Spes* (Pastoral Constitution on the Church in the
      Modern World)
LG   *Lumen Gentium* (Dogmatic Constitution on the Church)
PO   *Presbyterorum Ordinis* (Decree on the Ministry and Life of
      Priests)
SC   *Sacrosanctum Concilium* (Constitution on the Sacred Liturgy)
UR   *Unitatis Redintegratio* (Decree on Ecumenism)

--------------- **Scripture Abbreviations** ---------------

Acts	Acts of the Apostles	Lk	Luke
Bar	Baruch	Macc	Maccabees
Col	Colossians	Mal	Malachi
Cor	Corinthians	Mk	Mark
Eph	Ephesians	Mt	Matthew
Ex	Exodus	Pet	Peter
Ezek	Ezekiel	Phil	Philemon
Gal	Galatians	Prov	Proverbs
Gen	Genesis	Ps	Psalm
Heb	Hebrews	Rev	Revelation
Is	Isaiah	Rom	Romans
Jas	James	Sam	Samuel
Jer	Jeremiah	Tim	Timothy
Jn	John	Tit	Titus
Lev	Leviticus	Tob	Tobit

By
His Eminence
Donald Cardinal Wuerl
Archbishop of Washington

THERE IS PROBABLY NOTHING more visibly "Catholic" about the Catholic Church than the seven sacraments. The Church considers the sacraments to be such a part of her identity that she even calls herself a sacrament. What is a sacrament? And why are they so important? The answer to these questions lies at the very heart of the way in which we as Catholics understand who Christ is and how God chose to speak to us through Him.

Jesus truly saved us by deeds performed in His human nature, by His obedient love and patient endurance (cf. Heb 5:8) and by offering "his life as a ransom for many" (Mt 20:28). The Church solemnly teaches that the tragic consequence of Adam's sin had no other remedy than the merit of the one Mediator, our Lord Jesus Christ, who reconciled us to God in His blood.

Just as the Word took on a human body and became man, so the Church, the continuing presence of the Risen Lord, takes on the flesh of the liturgy to continue the work of Jesus. The Church, as did its divine founder, uses words, signs, symbols, and all forms of reality to accomplish its work. Its sublime mission is carried out by human agents. In doing their work, these people perform sacred ceremonies that are linked in what we call the sacraments with ordinary realities of human life: bread, water, wine, oil.

A sacrament is a sacred sign. In Catholic usage, the word "sacrament" usually more specifically indicates any of the seven sacraments in which visible realities are, by the will of Christ, made effective signs of His saving gifts. Because sacraments actually accomplish what they symbolize, they are unique signs. Because they put us in contact with God in a way that God's grace touches us, they are holy signs.

In the sacraments the Church can carry on the work of the Lord because Christ is the principal minister in each sacrament. Because it is Christ who works through the sacraments, they have a power and efficacy that do not depend solely on our disposition or the holiness of the human minister.

Since it is really Christ at work in a way that reflects His own Incarnation, the effects of the sacraments are intimately tied to the outward signs of each sacrament. The material, visible signs of the inner working of grace are called the *matter* of the sacrament, just as the words that proclaim the sacramental action are called the *form*. These human realities are necessary, together with faith, to produce the effect of the sacrament.

We shall look at each sacrament individually to listen and to try to hear what God says to us through that mystery of His presence.

Introduction

"I AM WITH YOU ALWAYS, till the end of the age" (Mt 28:20). This promise of Jesus is given to the disciples and to each one of us. While Jesus walked the earth, He worked many signs and wonders. His baptism in the Jordan begins His public ministry, as the Father reveals His beloved Son. Then, Jesus forgives sins and reconciles sinners. He heals the sick and raises the dead to life, and He feeds the multitudes with bread and with His word. On the eve of His Passion, Jesus institutes the Eucharist and the priesthood. And in the Paschal Mystery of His suffering, death, and resurrection, Jesus lovingly offers to the Father His own Body and Blood as a living sacrifice that lasts forever. After He ascends to His Father, the Holy Spirit is sent forth as advocate, guide, and sanctifier of the Church.

When we read or hear proclaimed the signs and wonders of Jesus, we may be inclined to think that these Gospel accounts are events of the past. We are amazed, as the first disciples must have been, by the mystery of Jesus' life, Passion, death, and resurrection. However, Jesus desired not only to heal, to forgive, to draw people to Himself in His day and time. His saving words and deeds were for all people of all time. And His saving work — that is, the fullness of God's revelation — will endure till the end of time.

The seven sacraments of the Catholic Church are the means by which Christ's redemptive work in His Passion, death, and Resurrection are present for all time and for all the faithful. The sacraments are the continuation, in every age, of the signs and wonders that Jesus worked while He walked on the earth some 2,000 years ago. We believe that "the sacraments are, as it were, arms of the Savior Himself by which He extends His action throughout place and time to give life, to bless, to renew, to heal, and to multiply the bread of life."

This short catechism on the sacraments invites you to deepen your understanding of the beauty and riches of the sacramental life of the Church. It is also an invitation to experience ongoing conversion and daily transformation of life through the graces of the Sacraments.

We begin with an introductory chapter on the seven sacraments of the Church so that your reflection on each of the sacraments is placed within the Catholic understanding of the nature of the liturgy, the Paschal Mystery of Christ, and the Church's sacramental life. Then, each of the seven sacraments is presented as the unique means by which the communion of the Church participates in the communion of the Blessed Trinity.

As disciples of Jesus Christ, we desire to know, love, and serve Him as members of His Body, the Church. We desire to live in the freedom and power of God's gift of love. With the help of this short catechism on the seven sacraments, you are invited to deepen your relationship with the person of Jesus Christ, through His living sacramental presence. The seven sacraments, instituted by Christ, are the means by which the Catholic Church offers to each person the life-giving love and presence of God — that is, grace. With this short catechism as a companion and guide, may your study and prayerful reflection be such a renewed moment of grace, so that you experience the abiding presence of Jesus Christ in His Church, in your life, and in the life of your family.

Chapter One

Liturgy: The Paschal Mystery and Sacramental Life

(CCC 1076-1130; 1179-1206; 1667-1676)

RELIGION, AT ITS CORE, is the quest for God. "One thing I asked the LORD, that will I seek after: that I may dwell in the house of the LORD all the days of my life" (Ps 27:4). In a special way, this personal quest for God is concentrated in prayer, and our personal prayer widens out to join with that of our fellow men in community prayer. When community prayer is the prayer of the living Church itself, gathering people into one in new ways, it becomes liturgy.

What is liturgy? Liturgy is "the full public worship performed by the Mystical Body of Jesus Christ, that is, by the Head and His members" (*SC 7*).

In this chapter we discuss the liturgy and Christ's presence therein, the Paschal Mystery, the meaning of "sacrament," and the use of sacramentals in the Church. In the chapters to follow, each of the seven sacraments instituted by Christ will be treated in detail.

Christ Present in Liturgy

Liturgical prayer is more than community prayer. The Second Vatican Council, in its *Constitution on the Sacred Liturgy*, showed anew how the realities of prayer and community — and sacramentality — converge in the liturgy. The Council did not speak of only a quest or of an encounter, but of a presence — that is, the presence of God in Christ in the liturgy. Indeed, we seek and find God only if He first comes to us. "In this is love, not that we loved God but that He loved us" (1 Jn 4:10). God, therefore, is present. It is we who are absent and must seek the encounter; the obstacles to be removed are in ourselves.

Christ is always present in His Church, especially in her liturgical celebrations. He is present in the sacrifice of the Mass, not only in the person of His minister, "the same one now offering, through the ministry of priests, who formerly offered Himself on the cross,"[1] but especially under the Eucharistic species. By His power He is present in the sacraments, so that when a man baptizes it is really Christ Himself who baptizes. He is present in His word, since it is He Himself who speaks when the holy scriptures are read in the Church. He is present, finally, when the Church prays and sings, for He promised: "Where two or three are gathered together in my name, there am I in the midst of them" (Mt 18:20).

— SC 7

Christ, then, is present even as His members gather together in communal prayer. In the liturgy, we see the Church assembled for its central purpose of worship. Here, the Head and members are gathered together before the Father. Here, we are enveloped by the covenant which God Himself has made, not with isolated individuals but with His people, united in Christ. Worship calls for the cooperation of the whole community, not merely as spectators but as participants.

Again, Christ is present in His word. It is "Christ Himself who speaks when the holy scriptures are read in Church" (*SC* 7). Because the Church wishes to make the riches of God's word more accessible, the celebration of every sacrament now begins with a Liturgy of the Word. In addition to readings, this liturgy includes pauses for meditation and prayer. The Liturgy of the Word is in effect a veritable school of prayer, an ascent through hearing, meditation, and devotion to intimacy. Since the quest for God is the heart at once of all prayer and especially of liturgy, prayer must indeed direct and form liturgical acts. Ritual without prayer is not liturgy.

In the liturgy, Christ is yet more wonderfully with us in His Eucharistic presence; and He is present in the saving power by which He acts in all the sacraments.

All these presences are part of what St. Paul calls the mystery of God, the mystery of Christ, the Paschal Mystery, or simply "the mystery" (cf. Col 2:2, 4:3).

The Paschal Mystery of Christ

"Our faith and the Eucharistic liturgy both have their source in the same event: Christ's gift of Himself in the Paschal Mystery," writes Pope Benedict XVI in his Apostolic Exhortation *Sacramentum Caritatis* (34). Indeed, the Church locates the center of the whole Christian religion in the Paschal Mystery. Christ redeemed mankind "principally by the Paschal Mystery of His blessed passion, resurrection from the dead, and glorious ascension, whereby 'dying, He destroyed our death and, rising, He restored our life' " (*SC* 5). [2] "The Church has never failed to come together to celebrate the Paschal Mystery: reading also 'in all the Scriptures those things which referred to Himself' (Lk 24:27), celebrating the Eucharist in which 'the victory and triumph of His death are again made present,'[3] and at the same time giving thanks 'to God for His indescribable gift' (2 Cor 9:15) in Christ Jesus, 'to the praise of His glory' (Eph 1:12), through the power of the Holy Spirit" (*SC* 6).

Only by realizing that in the liturgy the victory and triumph of Christ's death are made present can we understand two statements of the Second Vatican Council which might otherwise seem unintelligible: "The liturgy is the summit toward which the activity of the Church is directed; at the same time it is the font from which all her power flows" (*SC* 10) and, "It is the primary and indispensable source from which the faithful are to draw the true Christian spirit" (*SC* 14). If the liturgy were mere symbolic ritual, such claims could not be made for it. They are true only because the liturgy (which includes all the sacraments but is centered in the Eucharist) continues and makes present the Paschal Mystery of Christ.

The Unfolding of God's Plan

The Paschal Mystery is the heart of God's saving plan for us. This plan, of which Christ is the center and summit, unfolds gradually in the history of God's dealings with the human family and reaches its climax in bringing all things into one in Christ, uniting "all things in him, things in heaven and things on earth" (Eph 1:10).

God's saving plan culminates in "the fullness of time" (Eph 1:10) with the death and resurrection of Christ. By dying He destroys our death, and by rising He restores our life. At this point, a marvelous transformation takes place. What appeared at the time as a cruel and unjust execution is placed, by the epistle to the Hebrews, in its true perspective, in a cosmic liturgical setting. Calvary is seen as a towering mountain, a sanctuary where a new High Priest offers a sacrifice for all the nations of the world. The naked and crucified Servant, now replacing Aaron, appears as the High Priest of mankind according to the order of Melchizedek (cf. Heb 7; Gen 14:18):

> But when Christ appeared as a high priest of the good things that have come, then through the greater and more perfect tent (not made with hands, that is, not of this creation) He entered once for all into the Holy Place, taking not the blood of goats and caves but His own blood, thus securing an eternal redemption.... For Christ has entered, not into a sanctuary made with hands, a copy of the true one, but into heaven itself, now to appear in the presence of God in our behalf.
>
> — Heb 9:11-12, 24

The book of Revelation also describes this liturgy as the climax of history:

> And between the throne and the four living creatures and among the elders, I saw a Lamb standing, as though it had been slain.... "Worthy is the Lamb who was slain, to receive power and wealth and wisdom and might and honor and glory and blessing!"
>
> — Rev 5:6, 12

So Jesus crucified, then rising in the glory of the resurrection and ascending into the sanctuary of heaven, offers an acceptable sacrifice in a universal liturgy that joins all the redeemed to one another as they are united by Christ to Himself and to the Father.

Christ in Sacrament

This liturgy — this single sacrifice that redeems all, this most perfect act of worship — is then given to the Church. "Rightly, then, the liturgy is considered as an exercise of the priestly office of Jesus Christ" (*SC* 7). In this liturgy, Jesus Himself is the source of every sacrament, and of every visible sign of salvation. He *is* humankind's encounter with God. He is the Word made flesh (cf. Jn 1:14). "In Him we see our God made visible and so are caught up in love of the God we can not see."[4] He thus shows us in His person, by the humanity He has assumed, what sacrament is: God giving His life to us, God acting redemptively on us through His visible creation. Jesus further extended this principle when He established His Church, the fundamental sacrament, in which human beings of flesh like Himself — in fact, His brothers and sisters — are marked by the formative influence of the hidden Spirit. The other sacraments are means whereby Christ reaches out to humankind, and whereby the Church also, joined to Him as His Body, extends His healing and sanctifying action to all His members. As Pope Benedict teaches in *Sacramentum Caritatis:*

> The Church receives and at the same time expresses what she herself is in the seven sacraments, thanks to which God's grace concretely influences the lives of the faithful, so that their whole existence, redeemed by Christ, can become an act of worship pleasing to God (16).

The word "sacrament" comes from the Latin word for the Greek *mysterion*, the mystery of God in Christ in which St. Paul sees the vast unfolding plan and action of God among us (cf., e.g., Col 1:26). In this mystery, Christ poured into the Church the great sacrament that issued from him, all the riches of grace and truth gained through His death and resurrection. The Church, we have seen, was born "from the side of Christ as He slept the sleep of death upon the cross" (*SC* 5). The Preface of the Sacred Heart includes: "His wounded side, flowing with blood and water, is the fountain of grace renewing the Church with sacramental life."

The Seven Sacraments

Through the sacraments, the faithful cling to Christ and draw from Him this grace and life. The Church declares that in the New Law there are seven sacramental rites instituted by our Lord Jesus Christ.[5] These seven are: Baptism, Confirmation, Holy Eucharist, Penance, the Sacrament of the Sick, Holy Orders, and Matrimony.

Each of these rites has a visible material element or elements, like bread, wine, water, oil, or visible human actions. These material elements are illumined by sacred words to become signs of faith and instruments of Christ's own saving action on humankind. The visible sign of each sacrament symbolizes the gift of grace conferred by Christ in the sacrament.

These seven sacraments, then, are actions of Christ and of His Church. They are symbols and signs that we are blessed by God and saved by Christ's redeeming mercy. They are signs of faith by which we cling in worship to Christ to share the fruits of His Paschal gift; they are instruments by which Christ, through the liturgical acts of His Church, in fact confers the graces symbolized by the sacraments.

Pope Benedict XVI reminds us of the unity of the seven sacraments in these words:

> If the Eucharist is truly the source and summit of the Church's life and mission, it follows that the process of Christian initiation must constantly be directed to the reception of this sacrament . . . The Holy Eucharist, then, brings Christian initiation to completion and represents the center and goal of all sacramental life.
>
> — *Sacramentum Caritatis*, 17

The Material Signs

Jesus shows at once His power and compassion in meeting our human needs and aspirations, in a way we can see and understand. He further shows wisdom and understanding in choosing elements almost universally recognized by the religious spirit of created persons as having a character of quasi-sacredness; and this because of their connection with life, whose source is God. Christ often drew upon the powerful symbolic force of such material realities as water (cf. Jn 4:10-14) and bread (cf. Jn 6:27-58). True, these elements can be, and in paganism have been, deflected into superstitious and magical practices. But they can also be caught up in Christ's (and humankind's) effort to glorify the Father.

Sacraments are thus gifts of Christ by which He confers divine life and exercises divine power through expressive signs adapted to our human nature. In the sacraments, Christ reaches out to all people of every place and in every area. In His earthly life, Christ shared our finite limitation to one place and one time. Through the sacraments, the glorified Christ puts aside these limitations and draws us — by visible signs appropriate to our condition — to the new world of eternal life, already present but hidden. His sacramental action will continue everywhere until all His promises are fulfilled.

Sacramental Encounter

Our sacramental encounter with God through Jesus Christ is a veiled encounter. Nonetheless, it is also revealing, because the sacramental elements symbolize the character of God's action upon us. Water symbolizes cleansing and life. Bread and wine signify nourishment. Oil means healing and strength. And what they signify, according to Catholic teaching, is what Christ brings about through them. Hence, even though our meeting with God in the liturgy is veiled, it is nonetheless real. Through it we are drawn in all of the sacramental rites into the mystery of the Lord's death and resurrection and ascension.

In every sacrament we rise to God in praise, petition, and thanksgiving. At the same time, God comes to us bearing life and other gifts. One may think here of Jacob's dream of the stairway on which God's messengers were moving up and down (cf. Gen 28:12). Each liturgy is, as a prayer of the Christmas season expresses it, an "admirable exchange."[6]

Liturgical Celebration

Because sacraments are symbolic actions with very real effects, care must be taken to administer them validly — that is, in such a way that the full sign is present and its purpose is achieved. For all symbolic actions, even secular ones, concern for validity is basic. When one buys a house, the symbolic act of signing a contract has important rules for validity; it may be essential that the signing be witnessed or dated for the contract to be a valid instrument. If a symbolic action is not valid, it becomes useless and meaningless. It may reflect a sincere intent, but it does not achieve the desired effect.

Sacraments have conditions for validity. The sacraments are signs of faith and acts of obedience to Christ, so one may not arbitrarily choose signs other than those He appointed and entrusted to His Church. It is for the Church to state the conditions of validity for sacraments. This, the Church does.

For example, the Church, faithful to Scripture, insists that Baptism can be validly administered only with water, not with other liquids, and that only bread and the fruit of the vine, not other materials, can be validly used in the Eucharist. It is not that these material signs have any sacramental power in themselves. Their fruitfulness here comes from the passion of Christ and His present care. But in the sacraments, Christ works mighty deeds for the public good of the Church, and His deeds must be done faithfully in the Church if they are to be His saving actions.

It is true that God's generosity is not limited to the sacraments. If in good faith a minister should fail to administer sacraments validly, God is able to supply in other ways the needs of those who seek him. Still, a sacrament itself is simply not administered if the conditions established by Christ, personally or through His Church, are not fulfilled.

Sacraments are sacred actions, and the human minister should celebrate them with great faith and charity. As the Church has always taught, however, the validity of a sacrament does not depend on the worthiness of the minister. It is not from the goodness or power of human ministers that the faithful hope to draw the fruits of salvation, but from Christ Himself, who is always the principal minister of the sacraments. The efficacy of sacraments is drawn from Him; sacraments are basically actions of Christ. "When Peter baptizes, it is Christ who baptizes; when Paul bap-

The Church is responsible for reverent care of the sacraments. It makes laws for their licit celebration and for their proper reception, so that the reverence due these gifts and the good of the faithful may be preserved. Thus, the Church may insist on reasonable requirements of place and circumstances for these acts of public worship.

But far more is required in administration of the sacraments than observance of minimal demands for validity and lawfulness. Each sacramental liturgy should be fully celebrated as an act of worship:

> Pastors of souls must therefore realize that, when the liturgy is celebrated, more is required than the mere observance of the laws governing valid and licit celebration. It is their duty also to insure that the faithful take part knowingly, actively, and fruitfully.
>
> — *SC* 11

The hurried, lifeless observance of a bare rite is scarcely a celebration. Our liturgy commemorates and proclaims the death and resurrection of the Lord. The Church wants the faithful to take part "knowingly, actively, and fruitfully." It states that the nature of the liturgy calls for full, conscious, and active participation (cf. *SC* 14).

The sacramental rites, then, are not to be handled mechanically, but with faith and with joyful celebration. Past, present, and future come together in each rite. Every sacrament recalls the Paschal Mystery in which Christ won redemption; each symbolizes a grace He now confers; the sacraments point always toward the fullness of eternal life.[8]

tizes, it is Christ who baptizes; when Judas baptizes, it is Christ who baptizes."[7]

Certain human dispositions, made possible by grace, are necessary for valid reception of a sacrament. A context of faith and a personal willingness to accept Christ and receive the gift must be present in any adult who wishes to receive a sacrament effectively.

Sacramentals

As we have already observed, Jesus Himself designated the basic material signs around which sacramental celebrations revolve. The

Church reaches further into the material universe and appropriates many other objects — indeed, potentially all — into the direct service of God and as signs in His worship. These the Church calls sacramentals, distinguishing them by name so that they will not be confused with the signs that are Christ's sacraments. They differ in this: the spiritual efficacy of sacramentals depends on the faith and devotion of the users, whereas the sacraments are, as it were, arms of the Savior Himself by which He extends His action throughout place and time to give life, to bless, to renew, to heal, and to multiply the bread of life.

Many of the secondary signs — for example, the altar, the font, the sacred vessels — are also drawn directly into worship, supplementing the primary signs and forming with them a constellation of signs for each sacrament whereby the meaning of the sacrament may be revealed, expressed, and shared by the worshippers. It is the task of a full, conscious, and active participation to explore, even to exploit, these signs. All the riches of ritual language should be called upon to clarify and enhance these signs and thus to proclaim the mystery of Christ with fervor, conviction, and gladness.

In Sum: The Grain of Wheat

The Lord Himself gave us a description of the Paschal Mystery on the eve of His death and resurrection. It contains His theological explanation of what was about to happen, contained in an image drawn from nature.

> "The hour has come for the Son of Man to be glorified. Truly, truly, I say to you, unless a grain of wheat falls into the earth and dies, it remains alone; but if it dies, it bears much fruit."
>
> — Jn 12:23-24

Jesus Himself is the "grain of wheat" that dies in order to "bear much fruit." This fruit, issuing from the Paschal Mystery, comes to us in the sacramental liturgies.

The same law applies to His followers, who are also grains of wheat:

"He who loves his life loses it, and he who hates his life in this world will keep it for eternal life."

— Jn 12:25

So the Paschal Mystery becomes a way of life for all the followers of Jesus.

While we live we are always being given up to death for Jesus' sake, so that the life of Jesus may be manifested in our mortal flesh.

— 2 Cor 4:11

And it is to the sacramental liturgies, especially to the Eucharist, that we bring our own daily dyings and risings to be drawn into the Paschal Mystery of the Savior. In this way, we can also say with the Apostle:

In my flesh I complete what is lacking in Christ's afflictions for the sake of His body, that is, the church.

— Col 1:24

Discussion Questions

1. Discuss the importance of Catholic belief in the sacraments as the continuation of the presence and saving work of Christ Jesus. Discuss the relevance of this Catholic understanding of sacraments for the life of the Church and for your life of faith.
2. Based on your reading of this chapter, discuss reasons why the sacraments of the Church must be carefully administered and celebrated, so that the full sacramental sign is present and its saving purpose achieved.
3. Christ is present in the liturgy in manifold ways, as explained in this chapter. Share how you can deepen your sacramental encounter with Jesus Christ who is present in these manifold ways in the liturgy.

Additional References:

United States Catholic Catechism for Adults: Chapter 14 — "The Celebration of the Paschal Mystery of Christ."

Catechism of the Catholic Church, 1076-1130; 1179-1206; 1667-1676.

Pope Benedict XVI, *The Sacrament of Charity* (*Sacramentum Caritatis*). Post-Synodal Apostolic Exhortation, February 22, 2007.

Words to Remember...

❑ Christ redeemed humankind "principally by the Paschal Mystery of His blessed passion, resurrection from the dead, and glorious ascension" (*SC* 5).

❑ The heart of the liturgy is the Eucharistic sacrifice, or Mass, in which Christ is the chief priest, and the lamb of sacrifice; in it, the Paschal Mystery is made present and is celebrated.

❑ The seven sacraments are Baptism, Confirmation, Holy Eucharist, Penance, Anointing of the Sick, Holy Orders, and Matrimony; these sacraments are sacred signs, instituted by Christ, that truly confer the graces they signify.

❑ Care must be taken to administer the sacraments validly — that is, in such a way that the full sign is present and its purpose is achieved.

❑ Sacramentals (such as the altar, holy water, sacred vessels) are signs instituted by the Church; their efficacy depends on the faith and devotion of those who use them.

Endnotes to Chapter One

1. Council of Trent, Session 22, Sept. 17, 1562, *Doctrine of the Most Holy Sacrifice of the Mass*, ch. 2 (DS 1743).

2. The interior quotation is from the Preface for Easter in the *Roman Missal.*

3. Council of Trent, Session 13, Oct. 1, 1551, *Decree on the Most Holy Eucharist*, Ch. 5 (*DS* 1644).

4. *Roman Missal*, Preface I for Christmas.

5. Cf. Council of Trent, Session 7, March 3, 1547. *Decree on the Sacraments*, canon 1 on the sacraments in general (DS 1601).

6. Liturgy of the Hours, Feast of Solemnity of Mary, the Mother of God, the Octave of Christmas (January 1); first antiphon at vespers.

7. St. Augustine, *Tractatus in Ioannis Evangelium* 6.7 (ML 35.1428).

8. Cf. St. Thomas Aquinas, *Summa Theologica* II-II, 60, 3.

CHAPTER TWO

The Eucharist: Center of Life

(*CCC* 1322-1405; 1536-1589)

THE EUCHARIST IS AT the heart of the Church's life. In the Eucharist, Christ Himself is present to His people in the Paschal Mystery. Rich in symbolism and richer in reality, the Eucharist bears within itself the whole reality of Christ and mediates to us His saving work: "This most holy mystery," writes Pope Benedict XVI, "needs to be firmly believed, devoutly celebrated, and intensely lived in the Church" (*Sacramentum Caritatis*, 94). Further:

> At the Last Supper, on the night He was betrayed, our Savior instituted the Eucharistic Sacrifice of His Body and Blood. He did this to perpetuate the sacrifice of the cross throughout the centuries until He should come again, and so to entrust to His beloved spouse, the Church, a memorial of His death and resurrection: a sacrament of love, a sign of unity, a bond of charity, a paschal banquet in which Christ is received, the mind is filled with grace, and a pledge of future glory is given to us.
>
> — *SC* 47

This chapter concerns the Eucharist and its central role in Christian life, how it is the sacrifice of the new covenant and our saving food, its rich effects, and Christ's real presence in the sacrament.

The Eucharist: Center of Christian Life

The center of all Christian life is Christ Himself. By His Incarnation and work of redemption, we are healed and called to share in a new life, a life that binds us together as children of God and sharers in the life of the Trinity.

The Second Vatican Council rightly proclaimed that the Eucharistic sacrifice is the "source and summit of the Christian life" (*LG* 11). For in the Eucharist, Christ gives Himself to us, and we lay hold of him. The Eucharist is not merely a symbol and ceremony; it is the sacrament in which, most of all, the saving works of Jesus and the gifts of God are made accessible to men.

The existence of the local or the universal Church would be unthinkable without the Eucharist. "No Christian community can be built up unless it has its basis and center in the celebration of the Most Holy Eucharist" (*PO* 6).

The graced relationship begun in Baptism and strengthened in Confirmation is ordered to union with the Eucharistic Christ and a sharing in His saving sacrifice in the Mass. The Eucharist is the "medicine of immortality" which complements the healing effects of Penance and the Anointing of the Sick. Holy Orders confers a priesthood devoted to the altar of the Eucharist. Marriage symbolizes the union of Christ and Church which is the fruit of the Eucharist.

In the words of Pope Benedict XVI:

> It must never be forgotten that our reception of Baptism and Confirmation is ordered to the Eucharist... the sacrament of Baptism, by which we are conformed to Christ, incorporated in the Church and made children of God, is the portal to all the sacraments.... Still, it is our participation in the Eucharistic sacrifice which perfects within us the gifts given to us at Baptism. . . . The Holy Eucharist, then, brings Christian initiation to completion and represents the center and goal of all sacramental life (*SC* 17).

New Sacrifice of the New Covenant

Because the Eucharist is the most sacred presence of Christ and His Paschal Mysteries in the Church, it is both the "source and summit" (*PO* 5) of all the Church's ministries and apostolates. It threads a beauty, meaning, and purpose through all the varied activities involved in loving God, ourselves, and our fellow human beings. It offers a contact with the transcendent on which we can orient ourselves in the cosmic and timeless dimensions of our existence. In celebrating the Eucharist with and in Christ, the faithful are not only offered a share in His life; they are "invited and led to offer themselves, their labors, and all created things together with Him" (*PO* 4).

We have seen that it is by His cross and resurrection that Jesus brought us to newness of life. By these He inaugurated a new covenant in which He gives us His Spirit and makes us children of God, sharers of His life. We are made into a new community, a new people of God, able to worship God "in spirit and truth" (Jn 4:23), able as a family of God to join in the one sacrifice which is the hope and salvation of all forever.

These gifts of God are mediated to us chiefly through the Eucharistic Sacrifice. This memorial sacrifice was foreshadowed in the Old Testament, was instituted by Jesus, and is lived in His Church.

Foreshadowed in Old Testament

In one of the Eucharistic Prayers of the Roman liturgy, the history of salvation is recalled:

> Father...
> You formed man in your own likeness...
> Even when he disobeyed you and lost your friendship
> you did not abandon him to the power of death,
> but helped all men to seek and find you.
> Again and again you offered a covenant to man...[1]

In the ages before Christ's Incarnation, God enabled His people to seek Him and to find mercy. In various ways God taught them also to hope, and to offer sacrifices by which they acknowledged His lordship and bound themselves together as His people. Especially among God's chosen people, who were favored by the guidance of His special revelation, there were sacrifices that foreshadowed the one sacrifice that would truly merit salvation from all nations and all ages.

Every authentic sacrifice is a sacred offering directed to God alone, to acknowledge that He is lord of all. The very acknowledgment of His transcendent glory and supreme dominion helps the worshipper to draw near to Him who is greater than all. In many Old Testament sacrifices, a sacred meal was an element in the worship. In many sacrifices, part of the offering was destroyed to symbolize utter dedication to God; but part, made holy by its use in the sacrifice, was returned to the one offering it to be consumed. By this sharing, a kind of communion with God was accomplished.

From the first pages of Genesis onward, we see that the initiative to "share" was clearly and consistently God's. Again and again, God called men to sacred worship in which they might share His presence and His mercy. All these gifts of God were to be climaxed in the institution of the Eucharist.

With both Noah (cf. Gen 8:20, 9:9) and Abraham (cf. Gen 15:9, 18) covenants were made in the context of a food-sacrifice. Later, when their descendants refused to respect these covenants, God did not abandon them. Rather, He entered into the greatest of the Old Testament alliances in the complex of events known as the Exodus. Again, the covenant was associated with a sacred meal.

On the eve of the liberation of the chosen people from slavery under the Pharaohs, the Lord spoke to Moses and Aaron:

> "Tell all the congregation of Israel that on the tenth day of this month they shall take every man a lamb according to their father's houses... Your lamb shall be without blemish, a male a year old... You shall keep it until the fourteenth day of this month, when the whole assembly of the congregation of Israel shall kill their lambs in the evening. Then they shall take some of the blood, and put it on the two doorposts and the lintel of the houses in which they eat them. They shall eat the flesh that night, roasted; with unleavened bread and bitter herbs they shall eat it."
>
> — Ex 12:3, 5-8

There were further instructions:

> "In this manner you shall eat it: your loins girded, your sandals on your feet, and your staff in your hand; and you shall eat it in haste. It is the LORD's passover. For I will pass through the land of Egypt that night, and I will smite all the first-born in the land of Egypt.... The blood shall be a sign for you, upon the houses where you are; and when I see the blood, I will pass over you."
>
> — Ex 12:11-13

The meal was thus integrally connected with the circumstances of the liberation. The symbols of nourishment taken in community and of eating in haste while prepared for flight both captured in ritual what God was about to effect in history.

Added to this was the Lord's special command to repeat these ceremonies in the future:

> "This day shall be for you a memorial day, and you shall keep it as a feast to the Lord; throughout your generations you shall observe it as an ordinance for ever... for on this very day I brought your hosts out of the land of Egypt: therefore you shall observe this day, throughout your generations, as an ordinance for ever."
>
> — Ex 12:14, 17

Historically, the great Exodus covenant was completed only with the giving of the Law on Mount Sinai. Here the people received their obligations under the covenant, and Moses sealed the agreement by sprinkling an altar of sacrifice with calves' blood. Half the blood he sprinkled on the people with these words: "Behold the blood of the covenant which the Lord has made with you in accordance with all these words" (Ex 24:8).

The whole series of saving events was ritually preserved in the annual repetition of the Passover meal in what was called a "memorial feast." As generation after generation shared the paschal lamb and the unleavened bread, fathers told their children of the wonders Yahweh had worked on behalf of His chosen people. In this "memorial feast" they understood and celebrated far more than a community festival. The Passover meal was not looked upon simply as an opportunity to review past history. In this meal the people of God knew they were with their Lord, and they renewed the covenant He had made with them.

Instituted by Christ

At the Last Supper, the Lord instituted a new memorial sacrifice. The true "Lamb of God" (Jn 1:29) was about to be slain. By His cross and resurrection, He was to free not just one nation from bondage, but all humankind from the more bitter slavery of sin. He was about to create a new people of God by the rich gift of His Spirit. There was to be a new law of love, a new nearness to God, a new promised land. All was to be new, when God fulfilled the promises of the centuries in the Paschal mysteries. It was right, then, that there should also be a new memorial sacrifice, in which through all the ages, till the final fulfillment, God's people might be united to the saving deeds of this hour.

Jesus first carried out the rubrics of the Passover ritual. But in this holy night, He spoke of the new gifts to come, of which the treasures of the past were shadows and images. He promulgated the new law of the new covenant: "This is my commandment, that you love one another as I have loved you" (Jn 15:12). He spoke of the saving work He was about to do for them out of loving obedience to the Father (cf. Jn 14:31) and out of love for us (cf. Jn 15:13). Then, He made that redemptive sacrifice present in the institution of the Eucharist, in the memorial rite He would command them to perform always in His memory.

During the supper, at one of the ceremonial eatings of the unleavened bread, Jesus "took bread, and blessed, and broke it, and gave it to the disciples and said, 'Take, eat; this is my body'" (Mt 26:26). Picking up a ceremonial cup of wine, He gave thanks and passed it to His disciples, saying: "This cup which is poured out for you is the new covenant in my blood" (Lk 22:20). Finally, He commanded them: "Do this in remembrance of me" (1 Cor 11:24). Then, after singing songs of praise (cf. Mt 22:30; Mk 14:26), they walked down across the valley to where Jesus was arrested.

The interplay that took place in the Exodus between ritual and history was repeated at the New Pasch. Christ's crucifixion and resurrection, which constitute the sacrificial offering that frees us from sin, took place after the Last Supper, just as the flight from Egypt and the events of Sinai followed the first Passover meal. But Jesus' command to repeat this as a "memorial" of Himself established the Last Supper as the ceremonial setting for the representation of the events of our salvation. In this memorial sacrifice, the new covenant could and would be constantly renewed with every succeeding generation.

Like the Passover meal, this memorial sacrifice of the new law is both sacrifice and sacred meal:

Both sacrifice and sacrament pertain inseparably to the same mystery. In an unbloody representation of the sacrifice of the cross and in application of its saving power, the Lord is immolated in the sacrifice of the Mass when, through the words of consecration, He begins to be present in a sacramental form under the appearance of bread and wine to become the spiritual food of the faithful.[2]

As with many of the sacrifices of the ancient world, Christ's covenantal sacrifice was completed by the shedding of blood. This was not, as the New Testament reminds us, the blood of goats or calves, but rather the blood of the Priest Himself who presided in the cenacle and on Calvary (cf. Heb 9:12). Jesus died only once and shed His blood only once, but, because of the command for a memorial, that Blood is made available for all time.

"The institution of the Eucharist," notes Pope Benedict XVI, "demonstrates how Jesus' death, for all its violence and absurdity, became in Him a supreme act of love and mankind's definitive deliverance from evil" (*Sacramentum Caritatis,* 10).

Unity of Faith

With all the variety of ceremony in the Church, there is the wonderful uniformity of belief in the single reality that is celebrated. Together, the crucifixion and resurrection of Jesus are responsible for our redemption: "Jesus our Lord . . . was put to death for our trespasses and raised for our justification" (Rom 4:24-25). Unlike the repetitious sacrifices of the Old Law, the single sacrifice of Jesus' obedient death was completely sufficient in itself. As the epistle to the Hebrews stresses, He did not have to "offer Himself repeatedly, as the high priest enters the holy place yearly with blood not His own; for then He would have had to suffer repeatedly since the foundation of the world. But as it is, He has appeared once for all at the end of the age to put away sin by the sacrifice of Himself" (Heb 9:25-26).

The Eucharist and the Church

In describing the life of the early Church, Christian writers of that time gave special attention to the Eucharist. The Eucharist was the community's essential celebration; it signified, and kept most real, the presence of Christ in the community. In the Acts of the Apostles, St. Luke says of the converts at Jerusalem that they "devoted themselves to the apostles' teaching and fellowship, to the breaking of bread and the prayers" (Acts 2:42).

The phrase "breaking of bread" appears also elsewhere in the New Testament (cf. Acts 2:46; 20:7, 11; 27:35; 1 Cor 10:16) and in the oldest nonscriptural liturgical instructions we know of.[3] In describing the Church's activity in such terms, the writers were already witnessing to the essentially ecclesial nature of the Eucharist. The Church today remains the Eucharistic community. The celebration of the Paschal Mystery is the reason for the Church's existence. The Eucharist is "the most precious possession the Church can have in her journey through history."[4]

As Pope Benedict XVI writes in *Sacramentum Caritatis*:

> The Church "draws her life from the Eucharist"(31). Since the Eucharist makes present Christ's redeeming sacrifice, we must start by acknowledging that "there is a causal influence of the Eucharist at the Church's very origins" (32). The Eucharist is Christ who gives Himself to us and continually builds us up as His body . . . the Church is able to celebrate and adore the mystery of Christ present in the Eucharist precisely because Christ first gave Himself to her in the sacrifice of the Cross . . . so we too, at every celebration of the Eucharist, confess the primacy of Christ's gift.
>
> — No. 14

The liturgical form of Eucharistic worship developed in many places at the same time. There naturally arose a variety of forms, which reflected the cultures of the various faith communities as well as the different theological insights and devotional preferences of their people. This variety in external ceremonial still exists; each type is called a "rite."

In the western half of the Roman Empire, this variety eventually merged into a basic unity in the Latin rite. In the East, a variety of regional heritages was preserved. The two approaches resulted in a liturgical richness which the universal Church guards and treasures (cf. *OE* 1-6).[5]

The One Sacrifice

Jesus does not die and rise again every time the Eucharistic liturgy is enacted, but His one sacrifice is made present to all in every celebration of Mass. The God-Man instituted the Mass with an ecclesial dimension — its ability to be carried on everywhere in the Church — so that "the bloody sacrifice which was once offered on the cross should be made present, its memory preserved to the end of the world, and its salvation-bringing power applied to the forgiveness of the sins which are daily committed by us." When the Church celebrates the Eucharist, "the memorial of her Lord's death and resurrection," this central event of salvation becomes really present and "the work of our redemption is carried out."[6]

At Mass, as upon the cross, Jesus is the chief Priest as well as the Victim, giving unending and infinite praise and satisfaction to the Father. But in the Mass, His Church joins Him in the sacrifice. With him, the Church also performs the role of priest and victim, making a total offering of itself together with Him.[7]

Christ commanded His apostles to celebrate this sacrifice. "Do this in remembrance of me" (1 Cor 11:24). This is a sacred task: to act in the person of Christ, to be His minister, to speak words that make present the living Christ and renew the paschal mysteries. This can be done only at the will of Christ, by those whom He has empowered so to act as His ministers by calling them and sealing them in the Sacrament of Holy Orders. When, in the person of Christ, bishops and priests pronounce the words of consecration, the sacrifice of the new covenant is made present to the faithful in such a way that they, too, can participate in it.

Moreover, as Pope Benedict notes in *Sacramentum Caritatis*:

By His command to "do this in remembrance of me" (Lk 22:19; 1 Cor 11:25), He asks us to respond to His gift and to make it sacramentally present. In these words the Lord expresses, as it were, His expectation that the Church, born of His sacrifice, will receive this gift... the remembrance of His perfect gift consists not in the mere repetition of the Last Supper, but in the Eucharist itself, that is, in the radical newness of Christian worship (11).

Mass Offered for All

Priests are called to offer the Eucharistic sacrifice to the Father, with Christ, in the Holy Spirit, for the living and the dead, for the salvation of all, for the many needs of the people of God. Because the Eucharistic sacrifice is the supreme act of worship, it can be offered only to God.[8] The Church constantly draws her life from the redeeming sacrifices; she approaches it not only through faith-filled remembrance, but also through a real contact, since *this sacrifice is made present ever anew,* sacramentally perpetuated, in every community which offers it at the hands of the consecrated minister.

A Mass may be offered on the occasion of a saint's feast and give incidental honor to the saint. But the sacrifice of Christ is offered only to God, for He alone is worthy of this perfect adoration and praise. Masses may be offered for the needs of an individual person, living or deceased, but no Mass can be offered exclusively for such a limited intention. Every Mass is offered chiefly by Christ, and His ministerial priest must share His universal saving purposes. The Mass is offered to glorify God, to bring salvation to all, to make present and accessible the limitless riches of Christ.

Often the faithful ask that a Mass be said for a special intention of theirs: for the eternal rest of one who has died, for some spiritual or temporal need, or to express thanks to God. Ordinarily, they give a financial offering when they make such a request. When a Mass offering or stipend is given that a Mass be said for a special intention, it is in truth only a plea that part of the fruits of the Mass might come to one who is loved in Christ. A Mass offering or stipend is to be understood as an expression of a desire on the part of those who give it to participate more intimately in the Eucharistic sacrifice by adding "to it a form of sacrifice of their own by which they contribute in a particular way to the needs of the Church and especially to the sustenance of its ministers."[9]

Holy Communion

It is the privileged responsibility of the celebrant of each Mass to distribute the Sacrament to himself and the people. He may be assisted by other ordained ministers (bishops, priests, deacons) if they are available, or, when necessary, by auxiliary ministers (acolytes or specially appointed lay persons).

The Eucharist as received sacramentally is called "Holy Communion." The name is appropriate, since, as the word "communion" indicates, it is the sharing of a gift God gives to all; it is a coming into close union with Christ and with one's brothers and sisters in Him.

Because of its intimate connection with the sacrificial aspect of the Mass, Holy Communion is most fittingly received by those attending. One who has received Communion the same day may receive it a second time only within a Eucharistic celebration in which that person participates.[10] Catholics of the Latin rite have normally received the Eucharist only under the form of bread, though there are many occasions and circumstances in which they may receive under the forms of both bread and wine. Whether one receives under one species or both, one receives the whole Christ in Holy Communion.[11] This is true since, in the sacrament, it is the living, risen Christ who is present whole and entire under the appearance of bread, and also under the appearance of wine.

> To touch the Sacred Species and to share them with one's own hands is a privilege of the ordained, which indicates active participation in the ministry of the Eucharist. But it is clear that the Church can give such power to men who are neither priests nor deacons, of any sort, whether they are acolytes following their ministry, especially if they are destined for future ordination, or if they are other laypeople who have accepted the faculty from just necessity, but always after a suitable preparation.[12]

Participation

The ministerial priest, acting in the person of Christ, brings about the Eucharistic sacrifice and offers it to God in the name of all the people. The faithful, too, by virtue of their "royal priesthood" (cf. 1 Pet 2:9), join in the offering (cf. *LG* 10). They do this not only by the reception of Holy Communion, but by fully exercising their status as members of the Mystical Body, "offering the victim and themselves not only through the hands of the priest but also with him."[13]

> The celebration of Mass is the action of Christ and the people of God hierarchically assembled.... It is of the greatest importance that the celebration of the Mass, the Lord's Supper, be so arranged that the ministers and the faithful may take their own proper part in it and thus gain its fruits more fully. This is why Christ instituted the eucharistic sacrifice of His body and blood and entrusted it to His bride, the Church, as a memorial of His passion and resurrection. This purpose will be accomplished if the celebration takes into account the nature and circumstances of each assembly and is planned to bring about conscious, active, and full participation of the people, motivated by faith, hope, and charity. Such participation of mind and body is desired by the Church, demanded by the nature of the celebration, and is the right and duty of Christians by reason of their Baptism.[14]

Pope Benedict XVI observes that "some misunderstanding has occasionally arisen concerning the precise meaning of this participation" of the faithful in the Eucharist. The Holy Father points to the need for "authentic participation" when he writes:

> It should be made clear that the word "participation" does not refer to mere external activity during the celebration. In fact, the active participation called for by the Council must be understood in more substantial terms, on the basis of a greater awareness of the mystery being celebrated and its relationship to daily life.
>
> — *Sacramentum Caritatis*, 52

For fruitful participation in the Eucharist, certain personal conditions are required on the part of the faithful. Pope Benedict XVI further notes:

> One of these conditions is certainly the spirit of constant conversion which must mark the lives of all the faithful.

Active participation in the Eucharistic liturgy can hardly be expected if one approaches it superficially, without an examination of his or her life. This inner disposition can be fostered, for example, by recollection and silence for at least a few moments before the beginning of the liturgy, by fasting and, when necessary, by sacramental confession. A heart reconciled to God makes genuine participation possible. The faithful need to be reminded that there can be no *actuosa participatio* in the sacred mysteries without an accompanying effort to participate actively in the life of the Church as a whole, including a missionary commitment to bring Christ's love into the life of society (55).

Necessity of Communion

Jesus Himself stressed our need to receive Communion. "Unless you eat the flesh of the Son of man and drink His blood, you have no life in you" (Jn 6:53).

The divine precept does not state how often one must receive Communion. The Church requires that the faithful receive Communion at least once a year, in the paschal season, unless there is just cause for another time.[15] The Church speaks also of the duty to receive Communion when one is in danger of death.[16] But one who loves Christ naturally wishes to deepen one's friendship with Him by frequent reception of this sacrament.

Lawful Reception

To receive this sacrament worthily, one must be a baptized Catholic in the state of grace and believe what the Church teaches about the sacrament. One conscious of having committed a mortal sin must make a sacramental confession before approaching the Eucharist.[17] If one who has sinned gravely has a pressing need to receive the Eucharist and has no opportunity to confess, he should first make an act of perfect contrition, an act which includes in it a promise to confess as soon as possible.[18]

The New Testament reminds us of the grave duty we have to receive worthily:

Whoever, therefore, eats the bread or drinks the cup of the Lord in an unworthy manner will be guilty of profaning the body and blood of the Lord.... For any one who eats and drinks without discerning the body eats and drinks judgment upon himself.

— 1 Cor 11:27-29[19]

Reverence for the Eucharist reflects . . .

. . . an increased sense of the mystery of God present among us. This can be expressed in outward signs of reverence for

The Eucharistic Fast

As an outward and communal sign of this respectful awareness of whom it is that we receive in the Eucharist, and as a penitential preparation, the Church directs us to abstain from solid food and drink one hour before receiving Holy Communion. The sick and elderly and those caring for them are not obliged to fast. Drinking water and taking medicine do not break the Eucharistic fast.[20]

When instituting this milder form of Eucharistic fast, Pope Pius XII encouraged those of the faithful who can do so to observe the old and venerable form of the fast before Communion, that is, complete abstinence from all food and drink, even water, from midnight.[21]

Baptism also readies a person to communicate by conferring membership in the Church. Since the entire Eucharistic service is the most characteristic and important activity of the Church, it is an expression of a common belief, not only in the presence of Christ in the Eucharist, but in all that the Church is and teaches in the name of Christ. Fully participating in the sacrificial banquet is itself an act of faith; through it, Christians confirm and strengthen the belief that unites them to God and to one another.

It is because of this signification that non-Catholics may receive Communion in the Catholic Church only under exceptional circumstances. These are: (1) recipients must have the same faith in the Eucharist as is professed by Catholics; (2) they must have a deep spiritual need for the Eucharist; (3) they must have been unable, over a prolonged period, to communicate in their own church; (4) of their own accord they must request the sacrament of Communion. The local Catholic bishop is to pass judgment in each such case.[22]

the Eucharist . . . the importance of gestures and posture, such as kneeling during central moments of the Eucharistic prayer. Amid the legitimate diversity of signs used in the context of different cultures, everyone should be able to experience and express the awareness that at each celebration we stand before the infinite majesty of God, who comes to us in the lowliness of sacramental signs.

— Sacramentum Caritatis, 65

Symbol and Realities

Sacraments are outward signs instituted by Christ that symbolize what they effect and effect what they symbolize. This is true in a special way of the Eucharist when the faithful receive the sacrament at the table of the Lord.

Eucharist as Food

The most obvious sign of this sacrament is the image of nourishment. The elements used in the Passover meal were staples of the Palestinian diet in biblical times. Bread was available to everyone, the most common of foods. Wine was served as the normal table beverage, even in the homes of the poor.

The Western Church uses unleavened bread because unleavened bread was used at the Last Supper. The bread is to be of wheat only.[23] St. Paul saw unleavened bread as a symbol of purity and newness (cf. 1 Cor 5:6-8). Unleavened bread was also more quickly prepared than bread with yeast, and hence it fit in with the "pilgrim people" idea associated with the Exodus. We are a pilgrim Church, and we receive our spiritual Bread in a form that reminds us that we are still on the way to our promised land.

Wine was associated in popular thinking with joyful exuberance (cf. Ps 104:15). The reference to the Good Samaritan's pouring of wine on the injured traveler's wounds (cf. Lk 10:34) and St. Paul's advice to Timothy that a little wine is good for the stomach and recurring illness (cf. 1 Tim 5:23) suggest that the ancient world also considered wine to be somewhat therapeutic. This symbolism is retained in the Mass, where grape wine is still used.

The commands at the Last Supper to eat and drink fit in with the same symbolism. Jesus had even foretold the nourishment aspect of this sacrament in His preaching:

> "I am the bread of life; he who comes to me shall not hunger, and he who believes in me shall never thirst.... For my flesh is food indeed, and my blood is drink indeed."
>
> — Jn 6:35, 55

The Eucharist brings about the nourishing effect it symbolizes. This is achieved through the presence of Jesus Himself and the bestowal of grace on those who receive Him according to their individual needs and the needs of the community. Insofar as we have been wounded by sin, Christ and His power work in a remedial way; to the extent that we are making progress in holiness, He strengthens and fosters our growth.

> And, although it is true that the Eucharist always was and must continue to be the most profound revelation of the human brotherhood of Christ's disciples and confessors, it cannot be treated merely as an "occasion" for manifesting this brotherhood. When celebrating the Sacrament of the Body and Blood of the Lord, the full magnitude of the divine mystery must be respected, as must the full meaning of this sacramental sign in which Christ is really present.[24]

Symbol of Unity

The Eucharist symbolizes also the unity of the Church. Christ prayed for that unity at the first Eucharistic sacrifice (cf. Jn 17:20-21). The bread and wine He used were themselves symbols of unity; the family of God is to be gathered into one, as many grains of wheat are brought together to make bread and many grapes are brought together to make wine. An ancient Eucharistic prayer recalled this:

> As this broken bread was scattered over the hills, and then, when gathered, has become one mass, so may Thy Church be gathered from the ends of the earth into Thy kingdom.[25]

Unity is also symbolized by community sharing in the one Bread that is Christ:

> Because there is one bread, we who are many are one body,
> for we all partake of the one bread.
>
> —1 Cor 10:17

By the Sacrament of the Eucharist, "the unity of the Church is both signified and brought about" (*UR* 2). The unity of the Church, the Mystical Body of Christ, is effected chiefly by love:

> The liturgy inspires the faithful to become "of one heart in love"[26] when they have tasted their full of the paschal mysteries; it prays that "they may put into action in their lives what they have received with faith."[27] The renewal in the Eucharist of the covenant between the Lord and man draws the faithful into the compelling love of Christ and sets them afire.
>
> — *SC* 10

The union that worthy reception of Communion strengthens is, first of all, personal union with Christ. At the Last Supper, Christ said: "Abide in Me, and I in you. As the branch cannot bear fruit by itself, unless it abides in the vine, neither can you, unless you abide in Me" (Jn 15:4). But through union with him, we are bound together with one another, and thus made able to bear fruit for one another in works of love.

As a symbol of the unity of the Church, it is clear that:

> . . . since the Eucharistic liturgy is essentially an *actio Dei* which draws us into Christ through the Holy Spirit, its basic structure is not something within our power to change, nor can it be held hostage by the latest trends . . . the celebration of the Eucharist implies and involves the living Tradition. The Church celebrates the Eucharistic sacrifice in obedience to Christ's command, based on her experience of the Risen Lord and the outpouring of the Holy Spirit.
>
> — *Sacramentum Caritatis*, 37

Eucharist and Eternal Life

A third symbolism is that of our heavenly inheritance.

In the earthly liturgy, by way of foretaste, we share in that heavenly liturgy which is celebrated in the holy city of Jerusalem toward which we journey as pilgrims, and in which Christ is sitting at the right hand of God, a minister of the sanctuary and of the true tabernacle.

— *SC* 8

The entire Eucharistic service should symbolize the kingdom of God in its final fulfillment. Then the community of the faithful, gathered around the throne of the Father with their loved ones, will join with overwhelming gladness in Christ's perpetual praise and receive, as Abraham was once promised (cf. Gen 15:1), God Himself as their everlasting reward.

In the earthly celebration, there is an anticipatory experience of all these elements. Its peace, beauty, and order, though always imperfect in this life, are still a foreshadowing of the conditions of heaven.

Participation at Mass not only unites us with the living Church on earth but also with those who have gone before us, marked with the indelible character of faith.

Celebrating the Eucharistic sacrifice, therefore, we are most closely united to the worshiping Church in heaven as we join with . . . all the saints.

— *LG* 50

Most wonderfully of all, we experience a foretaste of the greatest reward, the presence of God within us. In the Eucharist we see him, albeit indistinctly with our weak faith, as in the dark metal mirrors of antiquity; yet it is the same Lord now whom we shall see in heaven "face to face" (1 Cor 13:12).

[For] man is created for that true and eternal happiness which only God's love can give . . . to move forward in the right direction, we all need to be guided towards our final goal. That goal is Christ Himself, the Lord who conquered sin and death, and who makes Himself present to us in a special way in the Eucharistic celebration.

— *Sacramentum Caritatis*, 30

Real Presence

The faith of the Church about the presence of Jesus in the Eucharist under the appearances of bread and wine goes back to the preaching of Jesus Himself, recorded in the Gospel of St. John. In the Eucharistic discourse after the multiplication of the loaves (cf. Jn 6:22-71), our Lord contrasted ordinary bread with a bread that is not of this world but which contains eternal life for those who eat it.

> "I am the bread of life. . . . I am the living bread which came down from heaven; if any one eats of this bread, he will live for ever; and the bread which I shall give for the life of the world is my flesh."
>
> — Jn 6:48, 51

The immediate reaction of the crowd to this claim was a mixed one. Some found this promise too much to believe. Their aversion to so puzzling a teaching was so strong that many disciples broke away and refused to follow Jesus any longer. Others, including the Twelve, did accept it. Even though such a notion was — for them as much as it was for those who rejected it — something beyond their personal experience, they gave their assent to His words because they recognized Jesus to be the Holy One of God, and they trusted in His assurance more than in the appearance of things (cf. Jn 6:69).

On one point, however, the two groups were in clear agreement. All of the hearers understood that Jesus was making a statement that was to be taken quite literally. Nor did He wish it to be understood in any other way. As Christian commentators have noted repeatedly, when the unbelievers walked away, Jesus did not retract the promise or try to change their understanding of His words. He did not call them back to say He had been speaking poetically or metaphorically.

We are constantly reminded in the liturgy that the Eucharist is "the mystery of faith." Pope Benedict XVI writes:

> With these words, spoken immediately after the words of consecration, the priest proclaims the mystery being celebrated

and expresses his wonder before the substantial change of bread and wine into the Body and Blood of the Lord Jesus, a reality which surpasses all human understanding. The Eucharist is a "mystery of faith" par excellence. The Church's faith is essentially a Eucharistic faith, and it is especially nourished at the table of the Eucharist. . . . Every great reform has in some way been linked to the rediscovery of belief in the Lord's Eucharistic presence among His people.

— Sacramentum Caritatis, 6

This mystery can be approached only "with humility and reverence, not relying on human reasoning, which ought to hold its peace, but rather adhering firmly to divine revelation."[28] Thus St. John Chrysostom follows the example of the faith of St. Peter (cf. Jn 6:68) in the Eucharist when he says:

Let us submit to God in all things and not contradict Him, even if what He says seems to contradict our reason and intellect. . . . Let us act in this way with regard to the mysteries, not limiting our attention to those things which can be perceived by the senses, but instead holding fast what He says. For His word can never deceive.[29]

Presence in Fullest Sense

The presence of Jesus in the Eucharist is not the only form of His presence within the Church, but the wonder of His Eucharistic presence is unique. Certainly, He is also with the Church in a special way as the Church believes, prays, and does works of mercy, and in its faith; He is with the bishops and priests of the Church when they preach God's word, govern His people, and administer His other sacraments. But the sacramental presence of Jesus brought about in the Mass has special claim to the description "real presence" — not because the other types of presence are not "real," but because it is "presence in its fullest sense."[30] The other six sacraments are rites in which the faithful encounter Christ in His action and power. Only the Eucharist, however, *is* Jesus Christ.

The way in which Jesus is present in the Eucharist cannot be explained in physical terms because it transcends the ordinary necessities of space and measurement. It is not as though Jesus took on a miniature body to be present in the Eucharist, or as though He were present in a natural way but hidden beneath a thin layer of bread and wine. It is a supernatural mystery that the Person who becomes fully present at Mass is the same risen Savior who is seated at the right hand of the Father. In becoming present on the altar, Christ's condition does not change. He does not have to leave heaven to become present on earth.

The same is true when many Masses are celebrated simultaneously. What changes is not Jesus, but the number of places in which He is present. When the Eucharistic liturgy is celebrated throughout the world, as it is daily "from the rising of the sun to its setting" (Mal 1:11), Jesus is not multiplied; nor is He diminished when His sacred Body and Blood are consumed in Holy Communion. Similar to the way the flame of the paschal candle is shared among the faithful on Easter night without becoming brighter or dimmer itself, and as the message of God in the Gospel is shared with all the members of a congregation at Mass without being itself enlarged or contracted, so Jesus' Body and Blood are not changed in any way in the continuous pulse of Eucharistic celebrations throughout the universal Church.

Meaning of Eucharistic Presence

The Eucharistic presence of Jesus is so rich in meaning that it can be spoken of in many ways. When the words of consecration are spoken over the bread and wine, there is a great change in meaning or significance — a "transsignification." That which had meant to us only earthly food and drink now means far more, and speaks to us the presence of Jesus. There is also a change in the purpose of what we see — a "transfinalization." The purpose of earthly bread is to minister to natural bodily life; when the words of Jesus have touched this visible gift of the Eucharist, its whole thrust and dynamism are different. It has become a food that nourishes the life of God in us and strengthens us for eternal life.

But deeper than all these changes, underlying them and their foundation, is the change in *being* — the "transubstantiation." The appearance of bread and wine "take on this new significance, this new finality, precisely because they contain a new reality."[31] Faith is concerned deeply with this reality; Jesus *is* here. He is present not merely spiritually, by His knowledge, His care, His activity, but He is present "in a unique way, whole and entire, God and man, substantially and permanently."[32]

Over what had been bread and wine, Jesus said: "This is My Body . . . This is My Blood."

> With firm faith in Christ, the Church has ever believed that what He gives us in the Eucharist is indeed His Body and His Blood. When His priest says His sacred words over the gifts, the bread and wine "have ceased to exist," and it is "the adorable Body and Blood of the Lord Jesus that from then on are really before us under the sacramental species of bread and wine."[33]

With Easter faith, we recognize that it is the Lord.

> Instructed in these matters and certain in faith that what seems to be bread is not bread — though it tastes like it — but rather the Body of Christ, and that what seems to be wine is not wine — though it seems so to the taste — but the Blood of Christ... strengthen your heart by receiving this Bread as spiritual food and gladden the countenance of your soul.[34]

The change that occurs when Christ becomes sacramentally present in the Eucharist is enduring because it is so radical, so real a change. After the consecration, Jesus remains bodily present as long as the appearances of bread and wine remain. Back in the fifth century, St. Cyril of Alexandria was once confronted with the false opinion that if a part of the Eucharist were left over until the following day, it would lose its power to sanctify. He rejected the opinion and replied with the belief that the faith has always proclaimed:

> For Christ is not altered and His holy Body is not changed, but the power and force and life-giving grace of the blessing remain in it forever.[35]

Adoration of the Blessed Sacrament

Faith in the enduring presence of Christ in the Blessed Sacrament prompted the gradual development of devotions to Christ in the Eucharist, even apart from Mass. "The worship of the Eucharist outside the Mass is of inestimable value for the life of the Church."[36]

Pope Benedict XVI speaks of the connection between the Mass and adoration and Eucharistic devotion in this way:

> In the Eucharist, the Son of God comes to meet us and desires to become one with us; Eucharistic adoration is simply the natural consequence of the Eucharistic celebration, which is itself the Church's supreme act of adoration . . . the act of adoration outside Mass prolongs and intensifies all that takes place during the liturgical celebration itself.
>
> — *Sacramentum Caritatis*, 66

In the earliest centuries of the Church, the chief reason for preserving the Sacred Species was to assist those unable to attend the liturgy, especially the sick and the dying. The Sacrament of the Lord was reverently taken to them so that they, too, could communicate.

With the passage of time, reverent reflection led the Church to enrich its Eucharistic devotion. Faith that Jesus is truly present in the sacrament led believers to worship Christ dwelling with us permanently in the sacrament. Wherever the sacrament is, there is the Christ who is our Lord and our God; hence, He is ever to be worshiped in this mystery.[37] Such worship is expressed in many ways: in genuflections, in adoration of the Eucharist, in the many forms of Eucharistic devotion that faith has nourished.

In the thirteenth century, when the charisms of saints like Francis of Assisi and Thomas Aquinas had intensified the Church's gratitude for the enduring presence of Jesus, the feast of Corpus Christi ("Body of Christ") was established. The popularity of this feast, with its joyful hymns and public processions, encouraged further developments of Eucharistic devotion.

The Blessed Sacrament is at times removed from the tabernacle in which it is ordinarily kept, and placed upon the altar for adoration. Usually the Host is placed in a monstrance, so that the Sacred Species can be seen by the faithful adoring their present but unseen Lord. These periods of exposition are sometimes extended into Holy Hours. Catholic parishes often celebrate Eucharistic Days, or the Forty Hours devotion, in which the Sacrament is exposed upon the altar continuously for a full day or longer, to intensify the Eucharistic life of the parish. When such exposition is terminated, the priest raises the Sacred Host before the people in blessing. From this closing act has come the name "Benediction of the Blessed Sacrament."

In some dioceses and certain religious communities, perpetual adoration is maintained before the continuously exposed Host. But every Catholic Church is a place in which the faithful are invited to worship the present Christ. Visits to the Lord in the tabernacle are still another form of devotion to the Real Presence that the Church warmly commends.[38]

Since the latter half of the nineteenth century, Eucharistic Congresses have drawn Catholics to international gatherings marked by liturgical functions, conferences, and other events. All these are designed to render our united gratitude and praise for the Father's great gift to us in this life: His beloved Son present among us under the appearances of bread and wine.[39]

Effects of Eucharistic Worship

All of life is to be transformed by authentic participation in the Eucharist. Pope Benedict XVI draws attention to the "all-encompassing effect of eucharistic worship" when he says:

> There is nothing authentically human — our thoughts and affections, our words and deeds — that does not find in the sacrament of the Eucharist the form it needs to be lived to the full. Here we can see the full human import of the radical newness brought by Christ in the Eucharist: the worship of God in our lives cannot be relegated to something private and individual, but tends by its nature to permeate every aspect of our existence. Worship pleasing to God thus becomes a new way of living our whole life, each particular moment of which is lifted up, since it is lived as part of a relationship with Christ and as an offering to God.
>
> — *Sacramentum Caritatis*, 71

―――――――――――― **Discussion Questions** ――――――――――

1. Read the Gospel accounts of the Last Supper (Lk 22:7-20; Mt 26:17-29; Mk 14:12-25). Discuss how the Eucharist instituted by Jesus at the Last Supper continues His saving work in every liturgy.

2. Discuss your understanding of Catholic teaching on the real presence of Christ in the Eucharist. Why is this teaching important for the life of the Church and the life of faith?

3. What relevance does the Eucharist have for your daily life and spiritual growth? Discuss the necessity of reception of Holy Communion as the sacramental means by which we deepen our friendship and communion with Christ and with His Body, the Church.

Additional References:

United States Catholic Catechism for Adults: Chapter 17 — "The Eucharist: Source and Summit of the Christian Life."
Catechism of the Catholic Church, 1322-1405; 1536-1589.
Pope Benedict XVI, *The Sacrament of Charity* (*Sacramentum Caritatis*). Post-Synodal Apostolic Exhortation, February 22, 2007.

Words to Remember...

Eucharist

❑ "Take, eat, this is My Body . . . This is My Blood of the covenant" (Mt 26:27-28).

❑ Jesus at the Last Supper changed bread and wine into His own Body and Blood, and commanded the apostles to do what He had done.

❑ At Mass, Christ through His priests changes bread and wine into His Body and Blood, and makes the sacrifice He once offered on the cross present for us.

❑ To receive Communion worthily is to have the sure hope of eternal life; we receive it worthily if we are in the state of grace and have faith in the Eucharist.

❑ We worship Christ in the Blessed Sacrament, for He remains there always as our Savior and our Friend.

❑ "The Blessed Sacrament contains the Church's entire spiritual wealth, that is, Christ Himself" (*PO* 5); hence, this sacrament is the source of all the Church's life and activity.

Endnotes to Chapter Two

1. *Roman Missal*, The Order of Mass, Eucharistic Prayer IV.

2. Pope Paul VI, Encyclical *Mysterium Fidei* (September 3, 1965) (EV 2.42 1).

3. Cf. *Didache* 14.1 (= ACW 6.23).

4. Pope John Paul II, Encyclical *Ecclesia de Eucharistia* (April 17, 2003), n. 9.

5. Cf. Congregation for the Sacraments and Divine Worship, Instruction, *Inaestimabile Donum* (April 3, 1980) (EV 7.288-323).

6. Council of Trent, Session 22, September 17, 1562. *Doctrine on the Most Holy Sacrifice of the Mass*, ch. 1 (DS 1740). Cf. Pope John Paul II, Letter to all the bishops of the Church on the mystery and cult of the Eucharist, *Dominicae Cenae* (February 24, 1980), n. 9 (EV 7.190-198) and Pope John Paul II, Encyclical *Ecclesia de Eucharistia* (April 17, 2003), n. 11.

7. Cf. Congregation of Rites, Instruction, *Eucharisticum Mysterium* (May 25, 1967), n. 3 (EV 2.1296-1303).

8. Pope John Paul II, Encyclical *Ecclesia de Eucharistia* (April 17, 2003), n. 12.

9. Pope Paul VI, Apostolic Letter on Mass stipends (June 13, 1974) (EV 5.534).

10. Cf. *Code of Canon Law*, canon 917. In danger of death one could, of course, receive Communion as Viaticum even if one had received Communion earlier in the same day; cf. the *Code of Canon Law*, canon 921, 2.

11. Cf. Council of Constance, Session 13, June 15, 1415, *Decree on Communion under the Species of Bread Only* (DS 1198-1200); Council of Trent; Session 21, July 16, 1562, *Doctrine on Communion under Both Species and Communion of Children*, ch. 1 and canons 1-3 (DS 1726-1727, 1731-1733).

12. Pope John Paul II, Letter to all the bishops of the Church on the mystery and cult of the Eucharist, *Dominicae Cenae* (February 24, 1980), n. 11 (EV 7.215).

13. *Roman Missal*, General Instruction, n. 62.

14. *Roman Missal*, General Instruction, nn. 1-3.

15. Cf. *Code of Canon Law*, canon 920.

16. Cf. *Code of Canon Law*, canon 921.1.

17. Cf. Council of Trent, Session 13, October 11, 1551, *Decree on the Most Holy Eucharist*, ch. 7 (DS 1647).

18. Cf. *Code of Canon Law*, canon 916.

19. Pope John Paul II has noted certain modern pressures toward unworthy reception of Communion and has urged pastoral care to guard the faithful from so great an evil; see Letter to all the bishops of the Church on the mystery and cult of the Eucharist, *Dominicae Cenae* (February 24, 1980), n. 11 (EV 7.208-209); Encyclical *Redemptor Hominis* (March 4, 1979), n. 20 (EV 6.1251-1256).

20. Cf. *Code of Canon Law*, canon 919.1 and 3.

21. Cf. Pope Pius XII, Apostolic Constitution, *Christus Dominus* (January 5, 1953).

22. Secretariat for Promoting Christian Unity, Instruction, *De Pecularibus Casibus Admitendi Alios Christianos ad Communionem Eucharisticam* (June 1, 1972) (EV 4.1626-1640).The National Conference of Catholic Bishops has issued the following "Guidelines for Receiving Communion":

— *For Catholics:* Catholics fully participate in the celebration of the Eucharist when they receive Holy Communion in fulfillment of Christ's command to eat His Body and drink His Blood. In order to be properly disposed to receive Communion, communicants should not be conscious of grave sin, *have fasted for an hour,* and seek to live in charity and love with their neighbors. Persons conscious of grave sin must first be reconciled with God and the Church through the sacrament of Penance. A frequent reception of the sacrament of Penance is encouraged for all.

— *For Other Christians:* we welcome to this celebration of the Eucharist those Christians who are not fully united with us. *It is a consequence of the sad divisions in Christianity that we cannot extend to them a general invitation to receive Communion.* Catholics believe that the Eucharist is an action of the celebrating community signifying a oneness in faith, life, and worship of the community. Reception of the Eucharist by Christians not fully united with us would imply a oneness which does not yet exist, and for which we must all pray.

— *For Those Not Receiving Communion:* Those not receiving sacramental Communion are encouraged to express in their hearts a prayerful desire for unity with the Lord Jesus and with one another.

— *For Non-Christians:* We also welcome to this celebration those who do not share our faith in Jesus. While we cannot extend to them an invitation to receive Communion, we do invite them to be united with us in prayer.

23. Cf. Congregation for the Sacraments of Divine Worship, *Instruction, Inaestimabile Donum* (April 3, 1980), n. 8 (EV 7.298); *Code of Canon Law,* canon 924.2.

24. Pope John Paul II, Encyclical *Redemptor Hominis* (March 4, 1979), n. 20 (EV 6.1254).

25. *Didache* 9.4 (= ACW 6.20).

26. *Roman Missal*, Postcommunion in the Easter Vigil Mass and the Mass of Easter Sunday.

27. *Roman Missal*, Prayer of the Mass for Monday within the Octave of Easter.

28. Pope Paul VI, Encyclical *Mysterium Fidei* (September 3, 1965) (EV 2.411).

29. St. John Chrysostom, *Homily on Matthew* 82.4 (MG 58.743).

30. Pope Paul VI, Encyclical *Mysterium Fidei* (September 3, 1965) (EV 2.424).

31. Pope Paul VI, Encyclical *Mysterium Fidei* (September 3, 1965) (EV 2.427).

32. Congregation of Rites, Instruction, *Eucharisticum Mysterium* (May 25, 1967) (EV 2.1309).

33. Pope Paul VI, *Professio Fidei* ("The Credo of the People of God," June 30, 1968) (EV 3.561).

34. St. Cyril of Jerusalem, *Catechesis* 22(myst. 4).9 (MG 33.1104).

35. St. Cyril of Alexandria, *Epistula ad Calosyrium* (MG 76.1075).

36. Pope John Paul II, *Ecclesia de Eucharistia* (April 17, 2003), n. 25.

37. Cf. Pope Paul VI, Encyclical *Mysterium Fidei* (September 3, 1965) (EV 2.433-434).

38. Cf. Congregation of Rites, Instruction, *Eucharisticum Mysterium* (May 25, 1967) part III (EV 2.1331-1341).

39. Cf. Pope John Paul II, Letter to all the bishops of the Church on the mystery and cult of the Eucharist, *Dominicae Cenae* (February 24, 1980), n. 3 (EV 7.163-164).

CHAPTER THREE

The Sacrament of Holy Orders and the Priesthood

(*CCC* 1533-1600)

Origin of Priestly Office

On the same first Holy Thursday on which He instituted the sacrament of the Eucharist, Christ conferred priesthood on the apostles: "Do this in remembrance of me."

In instituting the sacrament of the Eucharist, He created what would be a living re-presentation of His own death and resurrection. At the same time, He charged some to see that this sacred mystery would be performed thenceforth in His memory. Thus, the origin of Holy Orders lies in the will of Christ and His explicit acts on that first Holy Thursday.

Holy Orders and the great Christian paschal sacrifice are inseparable. Christ the Priest offered Himself for our salvation; the Eucharist is the continued re-presentation of that sacrifice; the priesthood is a special human participation in that divine work.

On the first Easter, the risen Christ breathed on His new priests and gave them the power to forgive sins: "Receive the Holy Spirit. If you forgive the sins of any, they are forgiven; if you retain the sins of any, they are retained" (Jn 20:22-23).

The new priesthood established by Christ was a "visible and external priesthood":

Sacred Scripture shows, and the tradition of the Catholic Church has always taught, that this was instituted by the same Lord our Savior, and that the power of consecrating, offering, and administering His Body and Blood, as also the power of forgiving and retaining sins, was given to the apostles and their successors in the priesthood.[1]

Holy Orders do not take their origin from the community...

... as though it were the community that "called" or "delegated." The sacramental priesthood is truly a gift for this community and comes from Christ Himself, from the fullness of His priesthood. This fullness finds its expression in the fact that Christ, while making everyone capable of offering the spiritual sacrifice, calls some and enables them to be ministers of His own sacramental Sacrifice, the Eucharist — in the offering of which all the faithful share — in which are taken up all the spiritual sacrifices of the People of God.[2]

The Sacrament of Holy Orders is rooted in Christ's Incarnation. In order to carry out the mission given Him by the Father, the Son of God became man. His work here culminated in His death, resurrection, and ascension. The priesthood, then, is based on the person and mission of Christ. Through the priesthood, He was to continue to make visible His saving action.

Identification with Christ

Central to an understanding of how Christ's work is transmitted to His Church is the notion of participation in the person and actions of Christ. Such participation touches the very life of Christ as shared through grace. By ordination, a believer is chosen from among the faithful to share more fully in Christ's priestly mission.

When a person is ordained a priest, he becomes a sign of God's presence and power in the world. His consecration represents Christ's total self-emptying, and also prefigures the day when Christ's kingdom will be fully realized. Since the priest is intimately identified with Christ, his priesthood is in some way a permanent part of his being. In philosophical terms, the priesthood is not merely a role one has, but it is an aspect of what one is. In theological terms, the priesthood is an irrevocable gift of God. "You are a priest for ever after the order of Melchizedek" (Ps 110:4).[3]

In explaining how the priest can function as Christ, the Church speaks of the priesthood as an identification with Christ on the most fundamental level. In their reception of orders, priests are "consecrated to God in a new way," and they become "living instruments of Christ the eternal Priest," so that they may be able to "carry on through the ages His wonderful work, which has with heavenly power reunited the whole society of men" (*PO* 12). The priestly office "is conferred by that special sacrament through which priests, by the anointing of the Holy Spirit, are marked with a special character and are so configured to Christ the Priest that they can act in the person of Christ the Head" (*PO* 2; cf. *LG* 10).

Pope Benedict XVI highlights the vital relationship between the sacrament of the Eucharist and Holy Orders in these words:

> The connection between Holy Orders and the Eucharist is seen most clearly at Mass, when the Bishop or priest presides *in the person of Christ the Head.* The Church teaches that priestly ordination is the indispensable condition for the valid celebration of the Eucharist . . . the priest is above all a servant of others, and he must continually work at being a sign pointing to Christ, a docile instrument in the Lord's hands.
>
> — *Sacramentum Caritatis,* 23

Christ lives and acts in many ways in the priest. The priest's identification with Christ is the theme of many works of the Fathers. St. John Chrysostom, for example, says that to disregard the teaching of the priest is to disregard God;[4] he also says that the hand of Christ moves through the hand of the priest, and that Christ's healing works are accomplished only through the priest.[5] The priest's power as "another Christ" is rooted in his unique ability to perform certain actions which are the works of Christ alone. "When you behold the priest offering the consecrated Bread, see in his hand the hand of Christ Himself."[6]

The priest's union with Christ is expressed by exercising the unique power that permits him to perpetuate Christ's work (cf. *LG* 10). This work is the essential work of the apostles: proclaiming the Gospel, gathering together and leading the community, remitting sin and anointing the sick, celebrating the Eucharist, exercising Christ's work of redeeming mankind, and glorifying God. In brief, those ordained to the priesthood are "sharers in the functions of sanctifying, teaching, and governing."[7]

Identification with Christ's Work

As Christ is teacher, witness, and means of saving sacrifice, so also is the priest. The source of all priestly existence and activity is Christ. Through the priest Christ makes His own priestly life and work present here and now.

The priest is differentiated from all others precisely by the way he is identified with Christ's unique work. The Church notes how certain powers identified with carrying on Christ's work were handed on. St. Paul clearly was conscious of his acting by Christ's mission and mandate (cf. 2 Cor 5:18-20; 6:4). This mandate was being passed on, with the obligation that it be handed on further. There is a warning: "Do not be hasty in the laying on of hands" (1 Tim 5:22). The two epistles to Timothy and the epistle to Titus express the sacramental aspects of the laying on of hands, and they point up the fact that ordination is not just a call to community service but a consecration.

Permanence of Priesthood

The priestly consecration is such that it cannot be lost. Once ordained a priest, a man remains a priest forever. The Sacrament of Holy Orders touches the very being of the recipient: he belongs to Christ in an enduring way:

> This special participation in Christ's priesthood does not disappear even if a priest for ecclesial or personal reasons is dispensed or removed from the exercise of his ministry.[8]

The permanence of the priesthood flows from the way in which the priest is united to Christ by his ordination. Christ's mission will be completed only in the glory of God's kingdom. Until the final realization of the kingdom, the priest remains the living sign and the promise of its completion in glory.

Thus ordination is an "eschatological sign" — that is, a sign pointing to the coming of Christ's kingdom. The priest's free giving of himself points to the day when Christ's kingdom will be fully realized. In that kingdom, all will freely give themselves irrevocably to Christ. By accepting priestly orders, the priest helps convert human freedom to God by uniting himself irrevocably with Christ in faith and grace. The priest is a sign of the kingdom to come and a pledge of the salvific presence of Christ.

> The Church has ever more closely examined the nature of the ministerial priesthood, which can be shown to have been invariably conferred from apostolic times by a sacred rite (cf. 1 Tim 4:14; 2 Tim 1:6). By the assistance of the Holy Spirit, she recognized more clearly as time went on that God wished her to understand that this rite conferred upon priests not only an increase of grace for carrying out ecclesiastical duties in a holy way, but also a permanent designation by Christ, or character, by virtue of which they are equipped for their work and endowed with the necessary power that is derived from the supreme power of Christ. The permanent existence of this character, the nature of which is explained in different ways by theologians, is taught by the Council of Florence and reaffirmed by two decrees of the Council of Trent. In recent times the Second Vatican Council more than once mentioned it, and the second General Assembly of the Synod of Bishops rightly considered the enduring nature of the priestly character throughout life as pertaining to the teaching of faith. [9]

To accept ordination, then, is to make a permanent commitment. But at times, the Church does permit priests to cease exercising their ministry. For serious reasons the Church may dispense them from the special priestly obligations, as that of celibacy and that of praying the Liturgy of the Hours daily. To some people, it may seem strange that the Church can permit a priest to leave his priestly commitment and enter marriage, while it does not permit a person in an unhappy marriage to leave the commitment and marry again. But the cases are different. The Church may dispense from its own law of priestly celibacy; it does not have the power to dispense from Christ's prohibition of divorce and remarriage. There is some likeness in the cases, however; all in the Church should pray that in every vocation, even in these times of widespread rootlessness, a spirit of faithfulness may grow.

Sacramental Ministry

A priest is preeminently a means of sacramental contact with Christ. The Christian meets God in the sacraments. And it is through the priest that Christ maintains His sacramental presence.

The priest is called to act in the very person of Christ.[10] In the Sacrament of Penance, he says: "I absolve you..." And in the Eucharistic sacrifice: "This is My Body... This is My Blood." In anointing the sick, the priest continues Christ's healing mission in a special manner. By administering the sacraments, the priest builds up the community of faith. By bringing human life into contact with divine life, he continues and extends Christ's work of establishing God's kingdom among us.

Priesthood of Christ Shared in Different Ways

All members of the Church share one faith and one mission, but the nature of a member's participation in the mission depends on the member's sacramental life and calling. By baptism, every Christian is joined to Christ and made a sharer in His divine life and mission. The sacrament of orders, however, makes one participate in Christ's mission in a unique way; it makes the recipient an authentic, authoritative, and special representative of Christ. For at the Last Supper, Christ instituted the ministerial priesthood as a distinct sacrament, and the priesthood of the ordained is different and distinct from the common priesthood of the faithful.

The priest, then, has a distinct role in the Church:

> Though they differ from one another in essence and not only in degree, the common priesthood of the faithful and the ministerial or hierarchical priesthood are nonetheless interrelated. Each of them in its own special way is a participation in the one priesthood of Christ. The ministerial priest, by the sacred power he enjoys, molds and rules the priestly people. Acting in the person of Christ, he brings about the Eucharistic sacrifice, and offers it to God in the name of all the people. For their part, the faithful join in the offering of the Eucharist by virtue of their royal priesthood. They likewise exercise that priesthood by receiving the sacraments,

by prayer and thanksgiving, by the witness of a holy life, and by self-denial and active charity.

— LG 10

St. Paul points out that the Holy Spirit is the source of the division of labor in the Church, and that the offices are quite distinct (cf. 1 Cor 12:4-11; Rom 12:4-8). The division of work follows a design set by God. Some are called to serve as priests, others to serve in other roles — and all are called to build up the Church of Christ (cf. 1 Cor 12:27-31).

Ministries within the Church

All mission with the Church is rooted in Christ's original sending of the apostles to teach His way to all (cf. Mt 28:19; Mk 3:14). All Christians share this task.

Within the Church, certain people must be chosen for particular functions. This is necessary in any organization. The selection and ordination of certain people are the means by which Christ's priestly work is carried on. Like all baptized persons, these people — bishops, priests, deacons — share in Christ's mission. Because they are set apart in a unique manner, they are appointed to share in Christ's work in a special way.

The Holy Spirit uses all ministries to build up the Church as a reconciling community for the glory of God and the salvation of all (cf. Eph 4:11-13). In the New Testament, ministerial actions are varied, and functions and titles are not all precisely defined. Explicit emphasis is given, however, to the proclamation of God's word, the safeguarding of doctrine, the care of the flock, and the witness of Christian living. By the time of the epistles to Timothy and Titus and the first epistle of St. Peter, some ministerial functions are more clearly discernible. This suggests that as the Church matured, the importance of certain functions caused them to be located in specific officials of the community. Here we can already see elements which remain at the heart of what we today call "ordination." The laying on of hands by a bishop seals a man as a priest. This ceremony in its essence is found in the pages of Scripture.

New Testament and Now

In the Church today, the sacrament of orders has three hierarchical grades, or orders: bishops, priests, deacons. Such offices were distinct in the infant Church, as we learn from the writings of the earliest Fathers of the Church.[11] In the New Testament itself, there is frequent mention of bishops ("overseers"), priests ("elders"), and deacons (cf., e.g., Phil 1:1; Tit 1:5-7). However, the Greek words for *bishop* and *priest* seem at times to have been used interchangeably. It is not altogether clear from the books of the New Testament that in ordaining their first associates to the ministerial priesthood the apostles distinguished the office of priest from that of bishop. It is possible that the distinction of orders appeared as the Church developed and it became useful to have not only ministers enjoying the fullness of the sacramental priesthood — that is, bishops — but also assistants to them, ministers having a real but more limited participation in the same priesthood. But the three orders of bishop, priest, and deacon did emerge in the early Church and have continued in it ever since.

It is quite clear from the New Testament that Christ chose leaders for His Church and gave them powers of teaching, ruling, and sanctifying. The apostles, it is true, had certain gifts and duties associated with their unique role as Christ's companions and as the foundation on which the Church was built at the start. But they had other roles that, by the will of Christ and in accord with the continuing guidance of His Spirit, were to be carried on in the Church through all the ages.

Two of these roles that were to continue in the Church were the ministry of forgiveness of sins (cf. Jn 20:21-23), and the offering of the Eucharistic Sacrifice. Other various powers that could be given men by God alone were to be continued in the Church. In the epistle to Titus, this companion of St. Paul who had been placed in charge of a local church is told:

> This is why I left you in Crete, that you might amend what was defective, and appoint elders in every town as I directed you...
> — Tit 1:5

While Paul and his associates were on their missionary journeys, they "appointed elders... in every church" (Acts 14:23). The
Greek word for "elder" is *presbyter*; this came to be the common
term for "priest."

As the Church developed, her priests continued to do divine
things, things that men may not do except with the authoriza-
tion of God. The Church taught that Christ had called men to
do these things, because He had chosen apostles and sent them
upon a mission that was to endure until He comes again. Those
the apostles chose to carry on their work were confirmed in Office
by Christ and the Holy Spirit. To those so appointed to rule the
Church in Asia Minor, St. Paul could say: "Take heed to yourselves and to all the flock, in which the Holy Spirit has made you
guardians" (Acts 20:28).

Thus, an essential part of the faith of the Church is conti-
nuity in mission. As Christ sent the apostles, so the apostles in
His name chose associates and successors, and they in turn laid
hands on others in Christ's name. By the guidance of the Spirit of
Christ, the hierarchical priesthood emerged in the Church, and it
continues at His will (cf. *LG* 18-22).

Orders are found in their fullness in bishops, in a secondary
manner in priests, and finally in the diaconate.

> Bishops enjoy the fullness of the sacrament of orders, and all
> priests as well as deacons are dependent upon them in the exer-
> cise of authority. For the 'presbyters' are prudent fellow work-
> ers of the episcopal order and are themselves consecrated as
> true priests of the New Testament, just as deacons are ordained
> for service and minister to the people of God in communion
> with the bishop and his presbytery. Therefore bishops are the
> principal dispensers of the mysteries of God, just as they are
> the governors, promoters, and guardians of the entire liturgi-
> cal life in the Church committed to them (*CD* 15; *PO* 2).

Bishops and Apostolic Succession

Bishops are successors of the apostles. By the will of Christ,
they carry on a task first done by the apostles, and they are always

needed in the Church. Apostolic succession, then, is a reality found in bishops, who trace their mission back to the apostles and to Christ.

> The mission entrusted by Jesus to the apostles is to last until the end of time (cf. Mt 28:20), since the Gospel which they have been charged to hand down is the life of the Church in every age. It was precisely for this reason that the apostles were concerned to appoint for themselves successors so that, as St. Irenaeus attests, the apostolic tradition might be manifested and preserved down the centuries.[12]

The third century theologian Tertullian concisely summed this up: "The Church from the apostles, the apostles from Christ, Christ from God."[13]

The incarnational character of the Church requires that Christ's powers be transmitted through individuals, not just through "the Church" in some abstract sense. The transmission of sacred power in the Church reflects the reality of the Incarnation and requires that real, living individuals in the Church be bearers of Christ's power.

Certainly historical, cultural, or social influences have shaped the style in which priestly office within the Church has been expressed. When the Church defines the priesthood as a sharing in Christ's saving mission, it prescinds from these historical variations. But there will be such accidental differences. The incarnational principle requires that any mission must be clothed in the cloth of the day. Christ's acceptance of the human condition sets the pattern for the Church.

Bishops are to the Church today what the apostles were to the early Christian community. Bishops are ordained to be the focal point of the local church and its source of unity. This unity appears especially when they offer the Eucharistic sacrifice in the midst of their priests and people. Bishops are ordained only by other bishops (cf. *LG* 21), and long-standing venerable tradition in the Church restricts to them also the ordination of priests and deacons. Bishops are also the ordinary ministers of the Sacrament of Confirmation, and — as the source and sign of the unity of the Christian community on the local level — they are the leaders in the Church's liturgical worship, just as they are the principal teachers within their dioceses.

> That divine mission entrusted by Christ to the apostles will last until the end of the world (cf. Mt 28:20).... Just as the role that the Lord gave individually to Peter, the first among the apostles, is permanent and was meant to be transmitted to his successors, so also the apostles' office of nurturing the Church is permanent, and was meant to be exercised without interruption by the sacred order of bishops.
>
> — *LG* 20

The Church teaches "that by divine institution bishops have succeeded to the place of the apostles as shepherds of the Church, and that he who hears them, hears Christ, while he who rejects them, rejects Christ and Him who sent Christ (cf. Lk 10:16)" (*LG* 20).

Priests

Bishops share their priestly orders with others:

> [Priests] are called to share in the priesthood of the bishops and to mold themselves in the likeness of Christ, the supreme and eternal Priest. By consecration they will preach the Gospel, sustain the people of God, celebrate sacred rites, especially the Lord's sacrifice.[14]

Priests are ordained to continue the saving action of Christ in and through the sacraments. A priest gathers the faithful for the Eucharistic sacrifice which only a priest can offer in the person and in the place of Christ. He forgives sins in the sacrament of Penance, again acting in the name and person of the Lord. His other specifically priestly functions are preaching, praying for the Church, anointing the sick, administering the other sacraments, and caring in every way for Christ's flock (cf. *PO* 2).

The priesthood must be viewed in the context of Christ and His Church. It is the Church which has primary responsibility for continuing Christ's work. Each bishop in charge of a local church is responsible for the sacramental life of his flock. He is in charge of a certain area of the Church, and within that area, usually a diocese, he is obliged to see that faith and Christian order are maintained. In charging others to help him, he gives them permission to exercise the orders they have received. When a priest is given this permission, he is said to "receive faculties." By his ordination a priest becomes a proper minister of the sacraments. But to perform priestly work, especially to hear confessions and to preach, he must also receive permission from the bishop in the area in which he is to function.

Women in the Ministry

The Church has always been blessed with women saints; the service of women in the Church has enriched the Christian community from earliest times. A number of women served Jesus in His ministry (cf. Lk 8:1-3), and Mary, His mother, shared in the saving work of Jesus more intimately than any other human person. In the life of the Church, women have been involved in countless indispensable ways: in teaching, in the care of the sick and the poor, and in administration, among other areas.

But women have never been ordained priests or bishops in the Church. Even the Blessed Virgin, whose role in the Church is more sublime than that of any other human person, was not called to any priestly office. Over the centuries, the Church has believed and taught that only male baptized persons may be validly ordained. It "has never felt that priestly or episcopal ordination can be validly conferred on women,"[15] and "this norm, based on Christ's example, has been and is still observed because it is considered to conform to God's plan for His Church."[16]

The sacrament of orders is not intended as a means of enriching the recipient, but for the good of the Church community. The Church has a duty to call to orders those — and only those — whom it judges, for the good of the family of faith, to accord with the will of Christ.

On May 22, 1994, Pope John Paul II wrote:

> [In order that] all doubt may be removed regarding a matter of great importance, a matter which pertains to the Church's

divine constitution itself, in virtue of my ministry of confirming the brethren (cf. Lk 22:32), I declare that the Church has no authority whatsoever to confer priestly ordination on women and that this judgment is to be definitively held by all the Church's faithful.[17]

Deacons

The diaconate is traditionally traced back to the apostles and to a time when the infant Church needed an expanded ministry;

> "Therefore, brethren, pick out from among you seven men of good repute, full of the Spirit and of wisdom, whom we may appoint to this duty...." These they set before the apostles, and they prayed and laid their hands upon them.
>
> — Acts 6:3, 6

The existence of the diaconate as a distinct office in the Church is often noted in Scripture (cf. Phil 1:1; 1 Tim 3:8-13) and is confirmed by the witness of the first Fathers.[18] Like the bishopric and the priesthood, the diaconate is a sacramental order and of divine institution;[19] it has an enduring place in the Church of Christ.

The title "deacon" comes from a Greek word meaning "service." The deacon gives service to the Church. Already in the time of the apostles, the richness of the ministry of the diaconate is suggested. Deacons serve at table, notably at the table of the Eucharistic meal. They are ministers of the charity of the Church (cf. Acts 6:1-4). They are witnesses to the faith, and defenders of it. Thus, the deacon St. Stephen became the first Christian martyr; and he proclaimed the faith with courageous eloquence and forgiving love before he was slain (cf. Acts 7). Deacons take part also in the Church's task of evangelization, as the deacon Philip did in Samaria (cf. Acts 8:4-13).

In the first centuries of the Church, the office of deacon was a permanent one of great importance in the community, but gradually, the scope of its ministry and influence declined. At length, in the Western Church, it became an order exercised by an individual for only a brief time; it was an office filled by one who intended shortly thereafter to become a priest. The Second Vatican Council called for a renewal of the permanent diaconate (cf. *LG* 29), so that this ancient vocation of service could again shine in the Church.

In our time, the Latin Church has decided to permit married men to become deacons. One effect of this decision has been that, in many places, an important ordained leader in a parish is drawn from the parish family itself. Still, the ancient witness to celibacy attached to Holy Orders remains. Anyone accepting the office of permanent deacon, if he is single, promises in the name of Christ not to marry; and if he is already married, he commits himself not to marry again should his wife die before him.

The ancient services of the deacon are continued in the Church today, with added tasks appropriate to our time. The deacon assists at the liturgy; he distributes Communion; he baptizes. He proclaims the Gospel and preaches. Deacons are invited to assist in many tasks of the Church: in catechesis, caring for the poor, and ministering to the sick (though it is the task of the priest to administer Penance and to anoint the sick). It is the deacon's office to assist bishop and priest in all the tasks of caring for Christ's flock.

Vocation and Priestly Qualities

Only those who are called by Christ should enter the priesthood. Christ directs His call, or vocation, to those He wishes. Young men are said to have the "signs" of a vocation if they are blessed with the health, intellectual ability, and strength of character required for the priesthood, and if they find in their hearts a desire to do priestly work for God's glory and the salvation of people. But the individual may only offer his service to the Church. The inner inclination must be confirmed by an ecclesiastical call. The Church has the task of confirming the reality of the vocation, and in Christ's name it ordains those selected. The choice is always Christ's. "You did not choose Me but I chose you" (Jn 15:16).[20]

No one can demand ordination. The imposition of hands in the Sacrament of Holy Orders is not a recognition of merit or a response to individual preference. It is the recognition of God's special call and the Church's unique role in salvation.

A priestly vocation is a call to a state of life requiring one to serve God for the spiritual welfare of others. Ordination is not a mere ceremony designating one for a particular position or profession in the Church. It is a sacrament which bestows not only the powers of administering the sacraments and preaching God's word, but also the grace that enables one to exercise these powers in a holy manner. The sacrament imparts a special grace of office.

One who accepts the call to serve as a priest must prepare himself to do priestly work. Like the secular professions, the priesthood requires natural aptitudes of body and mind. One who feels he has a vocation should also become aware of the qualities, particularly spiritual, that he must develop and maintain. Modeled on the example of the great High Priest, his must be a life of prayer, humility, and study. Furthermore, a priest gives up home and family life, because he has found a higher joy in devotion to God's work, in labor for the salvation of all.

Celibacy

When speaking of the sacrifices a man might make in order to follow him, Christ spoke of those who would give up wives and homes for the sake of the Gospel (cf. Mt 19:29). From the first days of the Church, there were priests who were celibate — that is, who did not marry — so that they might give their lives and hearts even more undividedly to the service of Christ (cf. 1 Cor 7:32-35; 9:5). However, different practices developed in different parts of the Church. In the Eastern Church, it was customary to permit the ordination of married men; in the West, it became the practice to ordain only those who felt they were able and willing to live celibate lives for Christ. Neither in the East nor in the West was a man permitted to marry after he had received Holy Orders.

Celibacy is loved in the Church for many reasons. It makes the priest more like Christ. St. Paul noted that it gives one great freedom in the service of Christ, and it deepens personal attachment to Him (cf. 1 Cor 7:32-35). Moreover, the Church desires priests — who preach the duty to bear the cross and to be obedient to God's commands even in the most difficult circumstances — to live in such a way that it is obvious that they are making great personal sacrifices for the Gospel. Priestly celibacy has also been called an eschatological sign, a sign pointing toward eternal life, for one who lives a celibate life in the world is living in a style appropriate to the reality of the next life, in which there will be no marrying (cf. Mk 12:25), and so manifests his faith in eternal life.

In recent years, many have urged that the Western Church drop its insistence on celibacy for priests, either to permit the ordination of married men or even to permit men already ordained to marry. This question was discussed at length at the Second General Assembly of the Synod of Bishops (1971), which concluded, "The law of priestly celibacy existing in the Latin Church is to be kept in its entirety."[21] This conclusion was confirmed by the Holy Father.[22]

Certainly, no human rights are violated by the requirement of celibacy for priests, for no one is required to become a priest. And the Church may rightfully retain the practice so commended by saints through the centuries, a practice that is so strong a support to the faith of the Catholic people, and continue to call to the priesthood only those who judge they can willingly live celibate lives for the sake of the kingdom.

Following the discussions of the Eleventh Ordinary General Assembly of the Synod of Bishops (2005), Pope Benedict XVI reaffirmed the beauty and the importance of a priestly life lived in celibacy as a sign expressing total and exclusive devotion to Christ and to the Church:

> It is not sufficient to understand priestly celibacy in purely functional terms. Celibacy is really a special way of conforming oneself to Christ's own way of life. This choice has first and foremost a nuptial meaning; it is a profound identification with the heart of Christ the Bridegroom who gives His life for His Bride. . . . Priestly celibacy lived with maturity, joy and dedication is an immense blessing for the Church and society itself.
>
> — *Sacramentum Caritatis*, 24

The requirement of celibacy is one the Church has power to relax should it judge this appropriate. But it is no arbitrary requirement. The New Testament message and the experience of the Church have shown how fruitful this charism, as lived by its priests, has been for the people of God.

Life of Prayer

The priest should be a man of prayer. On the day of ordination, the candidate receives the special obligation to recite the Liturgy of the Hours daily. The Church thus appoints its priests to a ministry of praise, adoration, petition, and thanksgiving. They are a "voice" of the Church, petitioning our heavenly Father to bless the whole world.

Meditation and reflection on what he is and what he is called to be should be part of every priest's life. Without deep spiritual convictions, without a spirit of prayer and sacrifice, he cannot lead the flock entrusted to his care to God. A priest, called to be always a man of God, must interpret the problems of the world and of his parishioners in the light of spiritual realities.

Witness

The priest's identification with Christ is clearly not limited to the dispensing of the sacraments in His name. The mission of the priest is also to represent Christ to the world and to be active in completing Christ's work in the world. In Christ's name he is to serve the word of God, bearing witness and evangelizing, lead the Christian community, and build Christian unity.

All these tasks of the priest are aspects of one integrated ministry. To preach Christ's message, to make His saving work present in the sacraments, and to build community in His name must all be parts of his ministry. Priests are to carry out the whole mission entrusted to them by Christ.

Service of Authority

In order to bring about unity, a priest is endowed with authority. Both evangelization and sacramental life demand a *diaconia* (service) of authority. The Church is the context for this priestly authority, and the Church's well-being limits and guides the exercise of it. Priestly authority at all times must work in harmony with the Church's purpose for the spiritual good of all believers and their unity in the Church.

The exercise of the *diaconia* of authority falls into two categories: the teaching of truth with authority, and the directing of the community in the path of unity. The first requires that the priest authoritatively interpret the word of God for his people in ways appropriate to his day. The second is centered in the priest's mission to maintain and build Christian community, acting with the authority conferred by Christ's wish that all may be one (cf. Jn 17:11).

The nature of the priest's authority to build community is conditioned by the nature of the community of faith that the priest undertakes to confirm and build.

> The proper mission entrusted by Christ to the priest, as to the Church, is not of the political, economic, or social order, but of the religious order (cf. *GS* 42); yet, in the pursuit of his ministry, the priest can contribute greatly to the establishment of a more just secular order, especially in places where the human problems of injustice and oppression are more serious. He must always, however, preserve ecclesial communion and reject violence in words or deeds as not being in accordance with the Gospel.[23]

Proclaiming the Gospel

A priest must continually announce the coming and presence among us of the kingdom of God. He is to pass on to others in word and deed the good news that he has received. Priestly witness takes place within the Church. It participates in the authenticity of the Church's witness, because, through the bishop, a priest shares in the call of the Church to spread the message.

The first "witnessing" task of the priest is to proclaim the Gospel. In accepting this task and carrying it out, a priest participates

Politics and the Priest

The priest's witness will always touch the political, social, cultural, and economic orders. His message must reach people where they are. The question is one of how he is to make his witness felt.

The work of the priest should affect notably the social and political life of the community. The priest is both a part of the political community and a spokesman for some of its most cherished principles. In his preaching, among other situations, he should make clear the moral imperatives contained in the Gospel message concerning the social order. Like all Christians, the priest has a responsibility to help make the political community just.

But the means a priest would use are ordinarily different from those appropriate for the layman, whose more immediate role it is to sanctify earthly structures. The extent of priests' engagement in secular political activity must be limited, and guided by the judgment of their bishops.[24] Similarly, while priests should preach on the public duties of Christians, they should not abuse their preaching role by insisting on a particular political, social, or economic option when there is more than one option in harmony with the Gospel.[25]

in the mission of Christ as the Truth, the Light of the world. Thus he brings people to faith, upon which they depend to reach God. A priest as witness is "guarantor" of the Gospel.[26]

The patristic tradition on witness is strong. St. Cyprian writes that priests are to witness to Christ in their words and deeds so that others may come to see and know Christ.[27] St. John Chrysostom notes that priestly witness must be "zealous" to be efficacious; he also notes the exclusive nature of a priest's work in devoting himself expressly to the eternal salvation of others.[28] St. Gregory the Great writes of the danger that arises when a priest devotes his time and energies to activities other than the care of the faithful and the works of the Church; regarding political engagement of a priest, he remarks that it leaves "his flock without a shepherd" and places the faithful in a position where they "cannot see the light of truth because the mind of their pastor is intent on earthly cares."[29]

The function of the witness is indispensable to faith. The world will not learn of the kingdom unless others tell them of it;

God's people must hear of grace, redemption, and eternal life if they are to know of them.

The priest, then, must testify not only to the Person of Jesus Christ, but to the content of the faith, carrying the words of life to those who are to believe and have no other way of coming to them, and testifying to the truth by words and acts.

In this aspect of his priesthood, the priest reflects the work of Christ. Jesus, speaking of His role as the witness of the Father, said He did nothing of His own authority, but said only that which He had been taught by the Father (cf. Jn 8:28). The priest as witness should absorb the message and remain obedient to it, passing it on as it is. The mission remains the same: to testify to the truth of God as revealed, that through the truth all may live.

Discussion Questions

1. Discuss how the Sacrament of Holy Orders is rooted in the Incarnation of Jesus Christ in the world. Why is the Sacrament of Holy Orders vital to the sacramental life of the Church?

2. How is the sacramental priesthood a unique participation in the priesthood of Jesus? Discuss the ways in which a priest becomes a sign of God's presence and power in the world.

3. Discuss the importance of each of the priestly qualities explained in this chapter. What are some concrete ways in which priests and laity support one another for the common good of the Church and the world?

Additional References:

United States Catholic Catechism for Adults: Chapter 20 — "Holy Orders."

Catechism of the Catholic Church, 1533-1600.

Pope Benedict XVI, *The Sacrament of Charity* (*Sacramentum Caritatis*). Post-Synodal Apostolic Exhortation, February 22, 2007.

Words to Remember...

Holy Orders

❑ Christ instituted the Sacrament of Holy Orders so that, through His bishops and priests, He might guard in the Church the Eucharistic presence, and confer on us His saving gifts.

❑ Holy Orders is conferred through the laying on of hands by bishops, the successors of the apostles.

❑ Only validly ordained priests can offer the Mass and celebrate the sacraments that Christ has reserved to their ministry.

❑ The priesthood belongs to Christ, and only those who are called by Him should seek priesthood; Christ's call is manifested by inner gifts and by the invitation of a bishop calling one to orders.

❑ Orders are conferred in varying degrees: the fullness of the priesthood is conferred on bishops; priests are given especially the power to celebrate Mass, to forgive sins, and to preach; deacons receive authority to proclaim the word and give service.

Endnotes to Chapter Three

1. Council of Trent, Session 23, July 15, 1563, *Doctrine on the Sacrament of Order*, ch. 1 (DS 1764).

2. Pope John Paul II, *Letter* to all the priests of the Church as Holy Thursday approaches (April 8, 1979), n. 4 (EV 6.1297).

3. In the ordination liturgy, Ps 110, including the verse quoted here, is recited immediately after the actual ordination.

4. Cf. St. John Chrysostom, *Homilia 2 in Epistulam II ad Timotheum* 2 (MG 62.610).

5. Cf. St. John Chrysostom, De *Sacerdotio* 3.6 (MG 48.643-644).

6. St. John Chrysostom, *Homilia 50 in Matthaeum 3* (MG 58.507-508).

7. Second General Assembly of the Synod of Bishops, *The Ministerial Priesthood* (1971) Part One, n. 4 (EV 4.1165).

8. Second General Assembly of the Synod of Bishops. *The Ministerial Priesthood* (1971) Part One, n. 5 (EV 4.1170).

9. Congregation for the Doctrine of the Faith, *Mysterium Ecclesiae* ("Declaration in Defense of the Catholic Doctrine on the Church against Certain Errors of the Present Day," June 24, 1973), n. 6 (EV 4.2586). Cf. Council of Florence, Bull, *Exsultate Deo* (November 22, 1439); Council of

Trent, Session 7, March 3, 1547, *Decree on the Sacraments*, canon 9 (DS 1609), and Session 23, July 15, 1563, *Doctrine on the Sacrament of Order*, ch. 4 and canon 4 (DS 1767 and 1774); Second Vatican Council, *LG* 21 and PO 2; Second General Assembly of the Synod of Bishops, *The Ministerial Priesthood* (1971) Part One, n. 5 (EV 4. 1169).

10. For an explanation of "in the very person of Christ," cf. Pope John Paul II, Letter to all the bishops of the Church on the mystery and cult of the Eucharist, *Dominicae Cenae* (February 24, 1980), n. 8 (EV 7.186).

11. Cf., e.g., St. Ignatius of Antioch, *Epistula ad Magnesios* 6.1 (MG 5.668 = ACW 1.70-71) and *Epistula ad Trallianos* 3.1 (MG 5.667 = ACW 1.76).

12. Pope John Paul II, Apostolic Exhortation *Pastores Gregis* (October 16, 2003), n. 6. Cf. *Adv. Haer.* III, 2,2;3, 1:PG7: 847-848.

13. Tertullian, *De Praescr. Haer.* XXI, 4.

14. Roman Pontifical, *Rite of Ordination of Priests*, n. 14.

15. Congregation for the Doctrine of the Faith, *Declaration on the Question of the Admission of Women to the Ministerial Priesthood* (October 15, 1976), n. 1 (EV 5.2115). Cf. also *Code of Canon Law*, canon 1024.

16. Congregation for the Doctrine of the Faith, *Declaration on the Question of the Admission of Women to the Ministerial Priesthood* (October 15, 1976), n. 4 (EV 5.2131).

17. Pope John Paul II, Apostolic Letter, *Ordinatio Sacerdotalis* (May 22, 1994) (EV 14.732-740).

18. Cf. St. Justin Martyr, *Apologia* 1.65 (MG 6.428=ACW 56.65); St. Ignatius of Antioch, *Epistula ad Philadelphenses* 4 (MG 3.700 = ACW 1.87).

19. Cf. Council of Trent, Session 23, July 15, 1563, *Doctrine of the Sacrament of Order*, chs. 2-3 (DS 1765-1766).

20. Cf. Pope Pius XII, Apostolic Constitution, *Sedes Sapientiae* (May 31, 1956).

21. Second General Assembly of the Synod of Bishops, *The Ministerial Priesthood* (1971) Part Two, n. 4 (EV 4.1219).

22. Cf. Rescript of the Audience given by the Holy Father to the Cardinal Secretary of State, November 30, 1971 (EV4.1134).

23. Second General Assembly of the Synod of Bishops, *The Ministerial Priesthood* (1971) Part One, n. 7 (EV 4.1175).

24. Cf. Second General Assembly of the Synod of Bishops, *The Ministerial Priesthood* (1971) Part Two, n. 2 (EV 4.1192).

25. Ibid. (EV 1195-1197).

26. Ibid., Part One, n. 4 (EV 4.1167).

27. Cf. St. Cyprian, *Epistula* 63.14 (ML 4.385-386 = ACW 46.105f.).

28. Cf. St. John Chrysostom, *Homilia 86 in Ioannem* 4 (MG 59.471-472).

29. St. Gregory the Great, *Regula Pastoralis* 2.7 (ML 77.39 = ACW 11.68-74).

CHAPTER FOUR

Sacrament of Initiation: Baptism

(*CCC* 1212-1314)

THREE OF THE SACRAMENTS — Baptism, Confirmation, and the Eucharist — are concerned with Christian initiation: "The three sacraments of Christian initiation closely combine to bring the faithful to the full stature of Christ and to enable them to carry out the mission of the entire people of God in the Church and in the world."[1]

As Pope Benedict XVI teaches us in *Sacramentum Caritatis:*

> It must never be forgotten that our reception of Baptism and Confirmation is ordered to the Eucharist. The Sacrament of Baptism, by which we are conformed to Christ, incorporated in the Church and made children of God, is the portal to all the sacraments...it is our participation in the Eucharistic sacrifice which perfects within us the gifts given to us at Baptism (17).

The Eucharist, which is the center of all sacramental life, has already been treated at length in an earlier chapter. In this chapter we discuss the Sacrament of Baptism.

Salvation History and Baptism

We may best approach the Sacrament of Baptism through the Holy Saturday Vigil liturgy, which is the masterpiece of the Church's liturgical catechetical teaching art. In the fullest sense, this liturgy is religious pedagogy. It goes beyond an abstract presentation of the Church's teaching by drawing on the prophetic symbolism of the Old Testament, which in turn leads to the teaching of the New Testament. Then all is brought together in a liturgy that richly expresses the meaning of baptism.

The first Scriptural reading of the Vigil liturgy is the creation story from the Book of Genesis (cf. Gen 1:1–2:2). It illustrates the power of God, culminating in the creation of human life. This narrative of divine power is seen here as a symbol of what St. Paul will call a "new creation," the creation effected by Jesus Christ through His passion and death

> Therefore, if any one is in Christ, he is a new creation; the old has passed away, behold, the new has come.
>
> — 2 Cor 5:17

> For neither circumcision counts for anything, nor uncircumcision, but a new creation.
>
> — Gal 6:15

This new creation actually takes place at the climax of the Vigil — in baptism.

The second reading (Gen 22:1-18) recounts Abraham's faith as shown in his readiness to sacrifice his son Isaac. This is a foreshadowing of Christ's sacrifice, from which Baptism, like all the other sacraments, receives its power. Isaac, spared, rose from the altar alive; Jesus died — the Father "did not spare His own Son" (Rom 8:32) — but rose again in a resurrection far greater than Isaac's.

The third reading (Ex 14:15–15:1) tells of the deliverance of the Jews at the Red Sea. This is linked with the account of the paschal sacrifice, anticipated on Holy Thursday. At this point, the concern is with the idea of deliverance through water, a necessary background for understanding the Lord's use of water and the power of baptism. Later, He will say to Nicodemus, "Truly, truly, I say to you, unless one is born of water and the Spirit, he cannot enter the kingdom of God" (Jn 3:5). Indeed, already in the Genesis account, the Spirit entered the waters creatively: "And the Spirit of God was moving over the face of the waters" (Gen 1:2).

The water is at once destructive, in Genesis, part of the wasteland and darkness, and also the source from which life arises. This double symbolism of water — death and life, destruction and salvation — becomes ever clearer in the history of Noah, which is alluded to in the fourth reading (Is 54:5-14). Water is used by God to destroy His enemies and save His friends. But the classic instance of this divine use of water is the passing of the Jews through the Red Sea, which, together with the paschal sacrifice, became central in Jewish life and salvation history, pointing forward to Christ "our paschal lamb" (1 Cor 5:7). Once more, God's enemies are destroyed by water, vindicating the divine justice, while in the same act His chosen people are delivered and pass over to the Promised Land.

The remaining readings (Is 55:1-11; Bar 3:9-15, 32–4:4; Ezek 36:16-17a, 18-28) are from the prophetic writings and point to the spiritual effects of baptism, still celebrating God's wonderful use of water, as Jesus would use it afterwards: "The water that I shall give him will become in him a spring of water welling up to eternal life" (Jn 4:14). The final reading, from Ezekiel, anticipates the "new creation" by promising a new heart and a new Spirit.

Thus the stage was set for "when the time had fully come" (Gal 4:4). When John the Baptist made his appearance in the Judean desert, he proclaimed a "baptism of repentance for the forgiveness of sins" (Mk 1:4). Jesus Himself, going down into the waters of the Jordan, brings this long, dramatic sequence of water-events to completion. Sinless Himself, He leads His people from sin through the waters of baptism to a new covenant with the Father.

St. Paul evidently had all this in mind when he wrote: "Do you not know that all of us who have been baptized into Christ Jesus were baptized into His death?" (Rom 6:3). But he has more in mind than the saving of the people at the Red Sea. He sees also the ultimate signification of baptism. Jesus Himself had said: "I have a baptism to be baptized with; and how I am constrained until it is accomplished!" (Lk 12:50; cf. Mk 10:38). And so Paul continues:

> We were buried therefore with Him by baptism into death, so that as Christ was raised from the dead by the glory of the Father, we too might walk in newness of life.
>
> — Rom 6:4

By the waters of baptism, sin and evil are destroyed and we rise to a new life, sharing in the resurrection of Jesus. "You have put off the old nature with its practices and have put on the new nature..." (Col 3:9). Indeed, "our old self was crucified with Him so that the sinful body might be destroyed, and we might no longer be enslaved to sin" (Rom 6:6). Then the whole Paschal Mystery, the dying and the rising of Christ as it envelops the baptized, is summarized by St. Paul in a passage read on Easter morning:

> If then you have been raised with Christ, seek the things that are above, where Christ is seated at the right hand of God. Set your mind on things that are above, not on things that are on earth. For you have died, and your life is hid with Christ in God.
>
> — Col 3:1-3

The Baptismal Liturgy

Against this background of salvation history culminating in Christ, we can appreciate the baptismal liturgy. Certainly in the case of adults, the preparation has started long before Easter; the Easter liturgy completes it. Easter is the most appropriate time for baptism and full participation in the Eucharist, since then, above all, we celebrate our sharing in the death and resurrection of the Lord. It follows that Lent is a most suitable time for preparing for baptism (or for preparing for renewal of baptismal pledges), as it was in the ancient catechumenate, the period of instruction prior to baptism. A major feature of the Church's *Rite of Christian Initiation of Adults*[2] is emphasis on the community aspect of baptism.

The Vigil itself begins with a Service of Light. From a new fire, the paschal candle is lighted; it stands for the risen Christ, His wounds now glorified: "The light shines in the darkness, and the darkness has not overcome it" (Jn 1:5). While the candle is carried in procession to the sanctuary, the light is gradually diffused as first the celebrant, then the ministers, and finally all others in the congregation light their candles from the paschal candle. The Easter Proclamation (*Exsultet*) is sung, all rejoicing in the victory of God's light at this climax of salvation history. Then come the scriptural readings described above.

The emphasis now turns to the joy of the resurrection. Altar candles are lighted, the *Gloria* is sung, church bells are rung. All is ready for baptism. First, the water is blessed with a prayer that sums up the salvation history just heard in the readings. The paschal candle is lowered into the water. Through the risen Christ, whom the candle signifies, the font will now become life-giving. The font, the womb of the Church, will bring forth children of God, as once more the Spirit of God is hovering "over the surface of the waters."

The baptismal promises are now pronounced. Then follows a profession of faith. Finally, there is the baptism itself. Those baptized are then anointed with chrism, recalling Christ's anointing by the Spirit, now shared by the new Christian. This foreshadows and anticipates the anointing of Confirmation, which may take place here. The baptized are thus admitted to God's covenanted people and will now be allowed to share in the "holy priesthood, to offer spiritual sacrifices acceptable to God through Jesus Christ" (1 Pet 2:5). The ceremony is completed by investing those who have been baptized with a symbolic white garment, the token of their baptismal innocence. They now are ready to share in the Eucharist in which we celebrate and renew the death and resurrection of the Lord.

Lent

The catechumens were (and are) an important part of the community during Lent. They vividly dramatize in their conversion and baptism the meaning of dying and rising with Christ at Easter. Nevertheless, Lent, as it developed, belongs to the whole community, for whom it has become an annual period of penance and renewal. Although Lent has not always consisted of forty days as it does now, the present number of days in Lent is based on the length of our Lord's own fast (cf. Mt 4:2).

Lent is a period for the instruction of catechumens, but it is a period for the baptized as well. The baptized Christian is encouraged to approach each Easter as one should when solemnly preparing for baptism. Today also, we have in Lent the opportunity to relive our baptism experience and deepen the realization of its meaning as we renew our baptismal vows at the Easter Vigil.

All this helps us understand the Lenten discipline of the Church today.[3] All acts of penance are part of that total conversion called for by baptism, a whole inner renewal leading one to think, judge, and arrange one's entire life under the impulse of the charity revealed to us in Christ. Acts of penance without this inner spirit are lifeless. Still, the inner spirit ought to be incarnated in deeds. There must be bodily penances — not because the body, so consecrated by Christ, is evil, but because we must take the flesh seriously and seek to liberate it also. To share Christ's cross is to be freed by Him ever more fully from the consequences of the Fall.

Christian penance traditionally involves prayer, fasting, and works of charity. In our times it may be appropriate, even necessary, in many instances to put less emphasis on fasting and more on the penance necessarily involved in faithful prayer and in doing charitable works. But the witness of Scripture and the life of the Church will not let us abandon corporal penances. Fasting and abstinence are encouraged in Lent, but Church law does not require a great deal of us in this regard. Specific regulations vary in different countries. In the United States of America, for example, all Fridays of Lent are days of abstinence — that is, days on which no meat is to be eaten — and Ash Wednesday and Good Friday are days of fast as well as abstinence. On fast days, one is to abstain from solid foods except at the one full meal and the two smaller meals permitted. Fasting binds those between the ages of 18 and 59; those who have reached the age of 14 are bound by abstinence. For sufficient reasons, the faithful may judge themselves excused or seek a dispensation from these particular regulations. But we can never be excused from the duty of doing penance. Because the Church is a family of faith, it is called in Lent to do penance collectively.

Fasting and abstinence are by no means the only types of penance.

Let us witness to our love and imitation of Christ, by special solicitude for the sick, the poor, the underprivileged, the imprisoned, the bedridden, the discouraged, the stranger,

Easter Customs

In Europe, the custom grew (and was sometimes transplanted to other areas) of bringing "Easter water" into the home to bless and renew everything. Food, which represents the resurgence of nature in the spring, was especially set aside to be blessed. All this is done to acknowledge the "new creation" spoken of by St. Paul and to rejoice that "the old has passed away" and "the new has come" (2 Cor 5:17).

Such simple customs have a large significance. If our Easter liturgy is to be really a joyous celebration, setting in high relief the culminating liturgy of the year, it must have a human dimension, must take root in our human lives.

Some have observed that although Easter is the greatest Christian feast, Christmas is in fact celebrated with greater joy. The reason seems plain. Christmas has more human resonances. There are family gatherings and reunions, children take the center of the stage, gifts are exchanged. To accomplish something like this for Easter, we need more than theological explanation. If a parish community could be brought to recognize Easter as the annual celebration of the baptism and First Communion of all the parishioners, then there might also be rejoicing and family gatherings, with sponsors as well as parents and grandparents.

the lonely, and persons of other color, nationalities, or backgrounds than our own.[4]

In the Scriptures, fasting is commonly associated with almsgiving (cf. Tob 12:8; Mt 6). When the well-fed fast, they are thereby able to share with the hungry, and this sharing by almsgiving is surely an act of love.

The Rite of Baptism

Baptism is, in fact, celebrated not only at Easter but at all times of the year. Still, the spirit of the Paschal Mystery must always penetrate its celebration. Baptism may be administered either by pouring baptismal water over the candidate's head three times, or by immersing the candidate three times in the baptismal water. While the water is applied, the celebrant speaks the baptismal formula: "N., I baptize you in the name of the Father, and of the

Son, and of the Holy Spirit." The water and the words symbolize the new life of the Trinity to which one is called, by sharing in the death and resurrection of Christ.

Bishops, priests, and deacons are the ordinary ministers of baptism. Anyone, however, even a non-Christian, can validly administer this sacrament by performing the rite with the serious intent to baptize in accord with the mind of the Church. Every Catholic should be able to administer this sacrament, should an emergency demand this. For such cases, the Church has prepared a suitable brief ceremony. If this cannot be used, it is sufficient to recite the Apostles' Creed (and even this may be omitted if necessary) and to pour water over the one to be baptized while saying the baptismal formula noted above. Children baptized in emergencies are to be greeted by the Church community with the special ceremonies prepared for the time when they are able to come to the church.

Each baptismal candidate should have at least one godparent, but may have a godfather and godmother. The godparent chosen by or for the one being baptized should be a mature person (ordinarily at least sixteen years of age), a Catholic living the faith, one who is able and willing to fulfill a role of spiritual concern for the one baptized. In special circumstances, as in the case of children of mixed marriages, a baptized and believing Christian of a separated community may serve as an additional witness to the baptism.[5]

The name to be given at baptism should not be out of harmony with the Christian calling of the person. The name of a saint is ordinarily given. Ideally, the saint whose name is chosen should become well known to the one baptized, as a patron and friend.

Effects of Baptism

The effects of baptism have been indicated in the scriptural passages cited and also in the liturgical signs of the Church described above. What remains is to bring these teachings together. In this we are aided by the *Rite of Baptism for Children*, for it crystallizes the Church's teachings on the sacrament. One of these, which is a basis for understanding all sacraments, concerns the manner of justification through grace. We are justified, the Church teaches, by God's grace and gifts, and this is "not only a remission of sins, but also the sanctification and renewal of the inner man."[6] This teaching refutes the error that justification, although accomplished by God's grace, is only an outward cloak. The Church insists that it is an interior sanctification, a true inward renewal accomplished "when, by the merit of the same most holy passion, the charity of God is poured forth through the Holy Spirit in the hearts (cf. Rom 5:5) of those who are justified and inheres in them."[7]

By baptism, people "are plunged into the Paschal Mystery of Christ: they die with Him, are buried with Him, and rise with Him" (SC 6). The ritual adds:

> Far superior to the purifications of the old law, baptism produces all these effects by the power of the mystery of the Lord's passion and resurrection.[8]

What are "all these effects" comprehended in the Paschal Mystery?

Dying with Christ

In our review of the Old Testament signs of baptism, we saw that water is at once destructive and lifegiving. So in baptism, there is a destructive process: "Those who are baptized are engrafted in the likeness of Christ's death. They are buried with him."[9] St. Paul explains:

> We know that our old self was crucified with Him so that the sinful body might be destroyed, and we might no longer be enslaved to sin.
>
> — Rom 6:6

How are we engrafted in the likeness of Christ's death? How are we buried with Him that we may pass from death to life? How do we put off the old self? By cleansing us from sin, the waters of baptism set us on a new way of life. When adults are baptized, their sins are forgiven even as they receive the new life of grace; for divine grace, in virtue of Christ's passion and death, has a forgiving and healing effect. Accordingly, baptism remits original sin and, for those baptized after infancy, also all personal sins that are sincerely repented of:

> "Repent, and be baptized every one of you in the name of Jesus Christ for the forgiveness of your sins; and you shall receive the gift of the Holy Spirit."
>
> — Acts 2:38

Converts to Christ need not submit themselves to the power of the keys by confessing their sins; in baptism, they are forgiven by an act of divine amnesty.

Since original sin involves all the members of our race, in this respect infants as well as adults must "die" with Christ and come to a new life of grace. This is made clear by the prayer of exorcism in the baptismal ceremony:

> Almighty and ever-living God,
> you sent your only Son into the world
> to cast out the power of Satan, spirit of evil...
> We pray for these children:
> set them free from original sin,
> make them temples of your glory,
> and send your Holy Spirit to dwell within them.[10]

Although the guilt of original sin is removed, some of its effects remain.

So the Church prays also:

> We now pray for these children
> who will have to face the world with its temptations,
> and fight the devil in all his cunning.[11]

St. Paul speaks of the effect of sin as feverish desire, or concupiscence, which he at times also calls "sin."

This inclination to sin remains in those who have been reborn in baptism. It is "left for us to wrestle with," but it "cannot harm those who do not consent but manfully resist through the grace of Jesus Christ."[12] This "wrestling," this agonizing struggle with our own desires, involves a lifelong sharing in the dying of Jesus.

God permits us to undergo this struggle that we may more fully share in the great work of our own redemption. Sometimes, this struggle seems almost too much for us. But steadfastness is made possible by the healing and quickening grace of the risen Jesus, which also assures victory to those who desire victory.

Rising with Christ

The baptized die with Christ only to rise with Him and share His life:

> They are buried with Him, they are given life again with Him, and with Him they rise again. For Baptism recalls the effects the Paschal Mystery itself, because by means of it men and women pass from the death of sin into life.[13]

It is the risen life of Christ we share. When St. Paul says: "I have been crucified with Christ; it is no longer I who live, but Christ who lives in me," he is writing of the risen life, for he adds:

> And the life I now live in the flesh I live by faith in the Son of God, who loved me and gave Himself for me.
>
> — Gal 2:20

The interior renewal we speak of is effected by this sharing in Christ's risen life.

Baptism makes us members of the Church. But to become a member of the Church is to be radically changed; it is to be grafted on the vine (cf. Jn 15:4-6) and joined vitally to the Body of Christ. Through an all-pervading bond of life, we become members of God's covenanted people. All this is effected in the Paschal Mystery: "This cup which is poured out for you is the new covenant in my blood" (Lk 22:20).

Children of God

"Baptism, the cleansing with water by the power of the living Word, makes us sharers in God's own life and His adopted children."[14] Baptism is both a rising with Christ and a new birth. As St. Peter wrote:

Blessed be the God and Father of our Lord Jesus Christ! By His great mercy we have been born anew to a living hope through the resurrection of Jesus Christ from the dead.

— 1 Pet 1:3

That we become children of God through baptism is told to us by Jesus Himself:

"Truly, truly, I say to you, unless one is born of water and the Spirit, he cannot enter the kingdom of God."

— Jn 3:5

Since Jesus Christ is "the only Son of God" (Jn 3:18), we receive our status by "adoption" (Gal 4:5). Still, as St. John assures us, this adoption is more than a legal process, as when children are legally adopted:

See what love the Father has given us, that we should be called children of God; and so we are.

— 1 Jn 3:1

Offspring share the nature of their parents. If we are truly children of God, we must in some way share in the nature and life of God. Scripture assures us that we do:

He has granted to us His precious and very great promises, that through these you may escape from the corruption that is in the world because of passion, and become partakers of the divine nature.

— 2 Pet 1:4

A Royal Priesthood

The first epistle of St. Peter is largely a meditation on baptism, its effects, and its practical implications. It brings many of the above themes together and yet says its own distinctive word: "And like living stones by yourselves built into a spiritual house, to be a holy priesthood, to offer spiritual sacrifices acceptable to God through Jesus Christ" (1 Pet 2:5). In studying the sacrament or orders we have seen the difference between the priesthood of the laity and the ministerial priesthood. St. Peter here speaks of baptism, by which all become worshippers of God in Spirit and in truth:

> You are a chosen race, a royal priesthood, a holy nation, God's own people, that you may declare the wonderful deeds of Him who called you out of darkness into His marvelous light. Once you were no people but now you are God's people.
>
> — 1 Pet 2:9-10

The apostle is recalling Exodus where the Jewish people were spoken of as a royal priesthood (cf. Ex 19:6), although only the Levites were specially designated for divine service.

In a similar way, while a new order of priests, sharing Christ's high priesthood, has been instituted to continue and renew His sacrifice, all the baptized are now called to join in worshipping God fully, consciously, and actively. As the context shows also, St. Peter is speaking here of the worship of the people not only in the sense of its liturgy but in the wider sense of embracing and sanctifying all the duties of life. The *Rite of Baptism for Children* brings these ideas together when it says:

> Baptism is the sacrament by which men and women are incorporated into the Church, built into a house where God lives, in the Spirit, into a holy nation and a royal priesthood. [15]

Baptism of Infants

So far, we have been concerned largely with adult baptism. Now we turn to infant baptism. [16] The practice of baptizing infants, questioned by some in the past, is again being questioned by some today. "Why baptize an infant, who has no understanding, who can make no personal commitment? Is it not unwise and even unjust for parents to predetermine the religion of a child, thus removing or diminishing later freedom of choice?"

The Church has solemnly defined the validity of infant baptism. [17] In fact, Church law commands Catholics to have their children baptized within the first weeks after birth. [18]

Almost from the beginning, if not from the very beginning of Christianity, infant Baptism was practiced when whole families were baptized. Among the "kinsmen and close friends" (Acts 10:24) whom Cornelius invited to hear St. Peter preach, and who were afterwards baptized with him (cf. Acts 10:48), there may well have been children. In any case, infant baptism clearly was practiced very early. Origen, writing in the third century, expressly states that the Church's tradition of baptizing infants came from the apostles.[19] St. Augustine cites the universal practice of infant baptism as evidence of the Church's traditional belief in original sin.[20]

The theological reason for infant baptism is given by Jesus Himself:

"Truly, truly, I say to you, unless one is born of water and the Spirit, he cannot enter the kingdom of God."

— Jn 3:5

There could be no stronger statement of the need for baptism. After the Resurrection, Jesus summarized the whole history of God's salvific power working through water when He placed all under the obligation of receiving baptism:

"Go into all the world and preach the gospel to the whole creation. He who believes and is baptized will be saved; but he who does not believe will be condemned."

— Mk 16:15

Moreover, would not parents converted to Christianity — especially when the conversion was a profound spiritual experience — desire to share this with their own children? Would they not be most anxious that their children also become citizens of God's kingdom and have their whole lives directed towards Him as their true last end and supreme good? Would they not also wish them to receive this orientation while they are most open to guidance from those they love?

Indeed, society itself is concerned with the birth of a child. A birth is a momentous event in the life of a family and of society, which is receiving a new member who may be creative or may be destructive.

Children born of Christian parents are introduced by baptism into the covenanted people of God. They are given a place, not only in their families, but in the community of the Church and in the universe; they are provided with a purpose, a key to the meaning of life, and a place in the economy of salvation in which these can be realized. The baptized child is introduced into "a chosen race, a royal priesthood, a holy nation, God's own people" (1 Pet 2:9). At baptism we are welcomed on earth by the very God who created us, received through the Son and at once made members of the Body whose Head is Christ.

The parents, in bringing their child to be baptized, are also acting as members of God's covenanted people; they are exercising their royal priesthood by introducing their child into God's holy nation.

The Necessity of Baptism

The Church, heeding the words of the Gospel (cf., e.g., Jn 3:3, 5), teaches that no one can enter the kingdom of heaven unless he or she is baptized.[21]

This insistence on the need for baptism for salvation may seem puzzling to many. Does it not follow that salvation is impossible for those who have never heard of Christ or baptism? This is by no means a new question. Nor is the answer new. Not all baptism is sacramental baptism with water. There is also "baptism of blood" and "baptism of desire."

Baptism of blood is received by dying for Christ. The Holy Innocents (cf. Mt 2:16-18) received such a baptism, as did the early catechumens who were martyred for Christ.

Baptism of desire has a far wider scope. It is most clearly present in those who explicitly wish to be baptized but who die before their intention can be carried out. Moreover, the desire for baptism does not have to be explicit. Baptism of desire can be present in one who, in response to God's grace, has faith in God and loves Him. Baptism of desire is certainly received by those who, implicitly or explicitly, desire baptism but for some reason are unable to receive it sacramentally. Even those who through no fault of their own do not know Christ and His Church may be counted as anonymous Christians if their striving to lead a good life is in fact a response to His grace, which is given in sufficient measure to all (cf. *LG* 16).[22]

Even this anonymous faith is implicitly directed toward the Church. There is only one Christ in whom people are saved. Those who love Him without knowing Him do wish in an obscure way to do His whole will. Implicitly, then, they do desire baptism, and this we call "baptism of desire."

The Baptismal Character

The Church teaches that Baptism, like Confirmation and Holy Orders, imprints a permanent character or sign.[23] St. Augustine, who introduced this use of the word "character" into Christian theology, took it from the mark by which soldiers were identified as belonging to a particular commander, owing him their allegiance. In the Scriptures the word used is "seal," which also marks or identifies. Yet the sacramental character is visible only in that it is conferred in a visible rite.

In order to understand the spiritual reality that the word "character" here expresses symbolically, we must note a significant difference between these sacraments and the others. The other sacraments may be received more than once, but Baptism, Confirmation, and Holy Orders may not. There is a reason for this. Apart from the grace that they confer, which can be lost through sin, the sacraments of Baptism, Confirmation, and Orders also have a lasting effect. This endures even if the recipient sins gravely. It remains in eternity. St. John in his vision of heaven sees an angel with "the seal of the living God," which was to be used in marking "the servants of our God upon their foreheads" (Rev 7:3). On the other hand, St. Paul speaks of our being sealed already in accepting the Gospel: "In Him you also, who have heard the word of truth, the gospel of your salvation, and have believed in Him, were sealed with the promised Holy Spirit" (Eph 1:13). The seal is also associated with anointing and the Holy Spirit (hence the use of chrism in the baptismal ceremony and in confirmation): "It is God who establishes us with you in Christ, and has commissioned us; He has put His seal upon us and given us His Spirit in our hearts as a guarantee" (2 Cor 1:21-22). Like St. John, St. Paul also sees this seal enduring into eternity: "Do not grieve the Holy Spirit of God, in whom you were sealed for the day of redemption" (Eph 4:30).

The character points to the stability and permanence of the Church. It cries out that God's gifts are enduring, and that He will continue to work His mercy in and through those He has chosen. "You are Christ's; and Christ is God's" (1 Cor 3:23). As priests share fully in the priesthood of Christ, and are ordained to make His sacrifice present everywhere, so by Baptism, all participate in a basic way in the royal priesthood of Christ, are designated for divine worship, and are rendered capable of offering their whole lives in union with His sacrifice. Even if they fail, they can be reconciled to the Church by the Sacrament of Penance without a repetition of Baptism.

Christ marks out His own. He has chosen us. We belong to him. He prays — indeed, He dies — that He will keep all of us:

> "Father, I desire that they also, whom you have given me, may be with me where I am.... It is the will of Him who sent me, that I should lose nothing of all that He has given me."
>
> — Jn 17:24, 6:39

The baptismal character is the sign at once of the Christian's permanent vocation, of his call by Jesus Christ, and, in the first place, of God's initial love.

Discussion Questions

1. Discuss the relationship between the Sacrament of Baptism, Lent, and the Easter Vigil.
2. In the Sacrament of Baptism, we are "plunged into the Paschal Mystery of Christ" through dying with Christ, being buried with Him, and rising with Him to new life. How do you experience the grace of baptism in your daily life as a disciple of Christ?

3. Discuss the meaning of each of the sacramental symbols and of the Rite of Baptism. How does your baptismal character encourage daily conversion of life?

Additional References:

United States Catholic Catechism for Adults: Chapter 15 — "Baptism: Becoming a Christian."
Catechism of the Catholic Church, 1210-1284.
Pope Benedict XVI, *The Sacrament of Charity* (*Sacramentum Caritatis*). Post-Synodal Apostolic Exhortation, February 22, 2007.

Words to Remember...

Baptism

❑ Baptism is a sacrament in which we are born again; in it we die with Christ and our sins are forgiven, and through it we rise to a new and divine life as members of Christ, sons and daughters of God, and heirs of everlasting life.

❑ Baptism is necessary for salvation; while baptism by water is the ordinary form, one who cannot receive this sacramental baptism may be saved by "baptism of desire" and "baptism of blood."

❑ In an emergency anyone, even a non-Christian, can baptize validly.

❑ Baptism, like Confirmation and Holy Orders, imprints a permanent character or sign; this identifies the recipient as belonging forever to Christ in a special way, and these sacraments may not be repeated.

Endnotes to Chapter Four

1. Congregation for Divine Worship, *Rite of Baptism for Children*, published by authority of Pope Paul VI, May 15, 1969, General Introduction, n. 2 (EV 3.1093). A second typical edition, published on August 29, 1973, lists several significant changes in the text on page 6.

2. Congregation for Divine Worship, *Ordo Initiationis Christianae Adultorum* (*Rite of Christian Initiation of Adults*), published by authority of Pope Paul VI, January 6, 1972; a new edition of the *Rite of Christian Initiation of Adults*, with modifications, was approved for use in the dioceses of the United States of America by the National Conference of Catholic Bishops on November 11, 1986, and was confirmed by the Apostolic See on February 19, 1988.

3. Cf. Pope Paul VI, Apostolic Constitution, *Paenitemini* (February 16, 1966) (EV 2.625-654).

4. United States National Conference of Catholic Bishops, Pastoral Statement on Penance and Abstinence, n. 15 (November 18, 1966).

5. On this paragraph, cf. *Code of Canon Law*, 873-874.

6. Council of Trent, Session 6, January 13, 1547, *Decree on Justification*, ch. 7 (DS 1528).

7. Council of Trent, Session 6, January 13, 1547, *Decree on Justification*, ch. 7 (DS 1530).

8. *Rite of Baptism for Children*, General Introduction, n. 6 (EV 3.1097).

9. *Rite of Baptism for Children*, General Introduction, n. 6 (EV 3.1097).

10. *Rite of Baptism for Children*, n. 49.

11. *Rite of Baptism for Children*, n. 49.

12. Council of Trent, Session 5, June 17, 1546, *Decree on Original Sin*, n. 5 (DS 1515).

13. *Rite of Baptism for Children*, General Introduction, n. 6 (EV 3.1097).

14. *Rite of Baptism for Children*, General Introduction, n. 5 (EV 3.1096).

15. *Rite of Baptism for Children*, General Introduction, n. 4 (EV 3.1095).

16. Cf. Congregation for the Doctrine of the Faith, *De Baptismo Parvulorum* (20 October 1980) (EV 7.587-630).

17. Cf. Council of Trent, Session 7, March 3, 1547, *Decree on the Sacraments*, canon 13 on the sacrament of Baptism (DS 1626).

18. Cf. *Code of Canon Law*, canon 867.

19. Cf. Origen, *In Romanos Commentarii* 5.9 (MG 14.1047). Cf. also St. Cyprian, *Epistula* 64.5.2 (ML 3.1018 = ACW 46.112).

20. Cf., e.g., St. Augustine's *Contra Iulianum Opus Imperfectum* 1.50 (ML 45.1073).

21. Cf., e.g., Council of Florence, Bull, *Exsultate Deo* (November 22, 1439) (DS 1314); Council of Trent, Session 6, January 13, 1547, *Decree on Justification*, ch. 4 (DS 1524), and Session 7, March 3, 1547, *Decree on the Sacraments*, canon 5 on the sacrament of Baptism (DS 1618). Cf. also *Code of Canon Law*, canon 849.

22. Cf. also Holy Office, Letter to the Archbishop of Boston (August 8, 1949) (DS 3866-3873).

23. Council of Trent, Session 7, March 3, 1547, *Decree on the Sacraments*, canon 9 on the sacraments in general (DS 1609). Cf. also *Code of Canon Law*, canon 849.

CHAPTER FIVE

The Sacrament of Confirmation

(*CCC* 1285-1321)

Divine Origin of Confirmation

Confirmation (like the Anointing of the Sick and Matrimony) is a sacrament about which we first learn in New Testament passages that speak of its use in the Church's liturgy. The Gospels contain no direct teaching on it, as they do on the Eucharist, Baptism, and Penance. When we first hear of this sacrament in the New Testament, it is already being administered — Christ having already ascended — in the infant Church. There are two places in the Acts of the Apostles where this is recorded.

> When the apostles at Jerusalem heard that Samaria had received the word of God, they sent to them Peter and John who came down and prayed for them that they might receive the Holy Spirit; for it had not yet fallen on any of them, but they had only been baptized in the name of the Lord Jesus. Then they laid their hands on them and they received the Holy Spirit.
>
> — Acts 8:14-17

The other passage is Acts 19:5-7.

That we learn of Confirmation through its liturgy is significant. This highlights the importance of liturgy as a means of knowing and transmitting religious teaching.[1]

Some Christians have denied the Church's firm teaching that Confirmation is a distinct sacrament instituted by Christ. Their denial could stem from a misinterpretation of the way in which faith is transmitted. Not everything the Church believes is explicitly articulated in abstract statements. The faith can be embodied in its attitudes and rites before it is explicitly formulated. This is certainly the case with the Sacrament of Confirmation (as well as the Anointing of the Sick and Matrimony). We must start with the sacrament as celebrated, then go back to the Gospels and to the Old Testament types to discover the rich meanings that have been brought together in this sacramental rite.

Anointing in Scripture

To the laying on of hands, described in the Acts of the Apostles, was added an anointing with oil. The oil of olives was a valued product in Palestine, as in most of the ancient world. Because of its many uses, it was also rich in significance. It was a food condiment, a beauty preparation, a medicine, an unguent for athletes, mixed with perfume for refreshment after bathing — and it was a sign of joy. It was the ordinary fuel for lamps, even in the sanctuary. A special sacred oil for anointing was prepared at the direction of Moses (cf. Ex 30:25 ff.). Aaron was anointed as high priest, and then Aaron's sons (cf. Lev 8:12, 30). Later Samuel anointed Saul as king, then David (cf. 1 Sam 10:1 f., 16:13 ff). In these instances, anointing brought the Spirit on those who received it, resulting in extraordinary actions: Saul prophesied and "the Spirit of the LORD came mightily upon David" (1 Sam 16:13).

Since Jesus in the line of David was the Messiah, He would certainly be anointed. So Isaiah had foretold (cf. Is 61:1), and this was the very prophecy that Jesus read and commented upon in teaching at Nazareth: "The Spirit of the Lord is upon me, because He has anointed me" (Lk 4:18). To be sure, Jesus was anointed directly by the Spirit, following His baptism by John. Yet the epistle to the Hebrews applies to Jesus, at least symbolically, a passage of the Old Testament which speaks of an anointing with oil:

> But of the Son He says, "You have loved righteousness and hated lawlessness; therefore God, your God, has anointed you with the oil of gladness beyond your comrades."
>
> — Heb 1:8-9; cf. Ps 45:7-8

Sacrament of the Holy Spirit

Thus, oil came to symbolize the coming of the Spirit, as a sharing of the gift sent first to the apostles. At times, the laying on of hands was absorbed into the act of anointing (as in the Eastern churches), and at other times both actions were retained distinctly. It should be noted that today in the Latin rite, "The sacrament of Confirmation is conferred through the anointing with chrism on the forehead, which is done by the laying on of the hand, and through the words *'Accipe signaculum doni Spiritus Sancti'* [Be sealed with the Gift of the Holy Spirit]."[2]

In the administration of the sacrament, olive oil perfumed with balsam is used (although other suitable plant oils and other fragrances are acceptable, according to availability). In consecrating this chrism, the bishop recalls that it takes its name from Christ, who is the Messiah, the "Anointed One." He goes on to pray that those who receive the sacrament may be given "the fullness of royal, priestly, and prophetic power." With chrism the Christian is, so to speak, "Christified."

Confirmation exists to extend to the Church of every time and place the gift of the Holy Spirit sent to the apostles on Pentecost. The Holy Spirit is the gift of Christ:

> "I will pray the Father, and He will give you another Counselor, to be with you for ever, even the Spirit of truth... the Counselor, the Holy Spirit, whom the Father will send in my name, He will teach you all things, and bring to your remembrance all that I have said to you.... But when the Counselor comes, whom I shall send to you from the Father... He will bear witness to me."
>
> — Jn 14:16-17, 26; 15:26

Christ's promise was fulfilled for the apostles on Pentecost:

> When the day of Pentecost had come, they were all together in one place. And suddenly a sound came from heaven like the rush of a mighty wind, and it filled all the house where they were sitting. And there appeared to them tongues as of fire, distributed and resting on each one of them. And they were all filled with the Holy Spirit and began to speak in other tongues, as the Spirit gave them utterance.
>
> — Acts 2:1-4

Marvels accompany the Spirit's coming — the mysterious wind, the tongues of fire, the gift of tongues, the bold proclamation, and the numerous conversions. But perhaps the most notable effect was the transformation of this frightened, cowardly group of men into inspired and fearless witnesses to their Lord's resurrection: "Their voice has gone out to all the earth, and their words to the ends of the world" (Rom 10:18; cf. Ps 19:4).

Confirmation is thus the sacrament whereby the apostles and their successors, by the laying on of hands and anointing with chrism, communicate to the whole Church and all its members the gift of the Spirit received at Pentecost. It is Pentecost extended throughout the world, perpetuated, and made ever present in the Church. It is a call to spread the kingdom of Christ, to spread the message of salvation.

Although any priest is authorized — as need urges and the Church delegates him — to administer the Sacrament of Confirmation, there is a special propriety in its being conferred by a bishop:

> The original minister of Confirmation is the bishop. Ordinarily the sacrament is administered by the bishop so that there will be a more evident relationship to the first pouring forth of the Holy Spirit on the day of Pentecost. After they were filled with the Holy Spirit, the apostles themselves gave the Spirit to the faithful through the laying on of their hands. In this way the reception of the Spirit through the ministry of the bishop shows the close bond which joins the confirmed to the Church and the mandate of Christ to be witnesses among men.[3]

Sacrament of Christian Maturity

In the early centuries of the Church, Confirmation was administered soon after Baptism. It became part of the Holy Saturday Vigil service following Baptism and preceding the Eucharist. Baptism, although a rebirth and a new creation, was assumed to require completion by the Spirit. Those who have been baptized still need the further pledge of guidance, inspiration, courage, and growth. Pope Paul VI writes:

The sharing in the divine nature which is granted to men through the grace of Christ has a certain likeness to the origin, development, and nourishing of natural life. The faithful are born anew by Baptism, strengthened by the sacrament of Confirmation, and finally are sustained by the food of eternal life in the Eucharist.[4]

The pope is here adopting the language of classical theology, especially that of St. Thomas Aquinas, who taught that the divine life of grace in which the Christian shares parallels the stages of human growth.[5] The three sacraments of initiation give birth, growth, and nourishment to this life. Penance and Anointing are for its healing and renewal. Marriage and Holy Orders are concerned with its continuance and transmission.

Anthropologists studying the ritual behavior of various peoples have arrived at a view of ritual that confirms the teaching of St. Thomas in a remarkable way. They find that religion, utilizing ritual, intervenes in life at certain critical moments and periods of its development. Birth is a critical time; adolescence is another; so likewise are marriage, sickness, and death. The Christian sacraments correspond with such critical times and help both individuals and the community through them. Once again, we see how the Christian religion responds also to our deepest human needs.

There is, however, some uncertainty about the place of Confirmation in this process of human development. Some would wish to see in Confirmation a sacramental sign of coming to spiritual maturity or of adult commitment to Christ. In this, they are supported by the New Testament examples of confirming adults. They also seem to be supported by the teaching that Confirmation confers strength and belongs to Christian growth.

On the other hand, precisely because Confirmation is a sacrament of initiation following Baptism, Eastern Catholics confirm even infants after their baptism. Others are concerned that Confirmation, because it is a sacrament of initiation, should at least precede full participation in the Eucharist, which is the climax of initiation. Some liturgical considerations, therefore, seem to favor early Confirmation; some psychological factors seem to urge postponement until at least the threshold of maturity.

The Holy See has left the matter somewhat open. The *Rite of Confirmation* states that, with regard to children in the Latin Church, "the administration of Confirmation is generally postponed until about the seventh year" yet allows that it may, for pastoral reasons, be postponed to "a more mature age."[6] In many places, the tendency is to postpone Confirmation at least until early adolescence. If we see the Christian life as a whole, progressing from rebirth to mature manhood in Christ (cf. Eph 4:13), there is no difficulty in regarding Confirmation, even when administered in adolescence or later, as a sacrament of initiation. Amidst variations in pastoral practice, the key is to consider "which practice better enables the faithful to put the sacrament of the Eucharist at the center, as the goal of the whole process of initiation" (Pope Benedict XVI, *Sacramentum Caritatis*, 18).

The sponsor for Confirmation should be like the godparent chosen for Baptism. In fact, it is appropriate that the same person be used.[7]

Lasting Effects of Confirmation

Confirmation implies growth, and it is a continual challenge to the recipient to cultivate growth. Life is required for this growth, and the recipient must be in the state of grace. Yet Confirmation cannot be counted on to produce instantaneous growth; nor is it intended to do this. As one of the sacraments which are administered to a person only once, and whose effect is therefore permanent, Confirmation confers a permanent character. This is shown by the words with which it is administered: "Be sealed with the gift of the Holy Spirit." We have heard St. Paul speak of this seal; his words to the Corinthians, already quoted above, seem especially applicable to Confirmation:

> It is God who establishes us with you in Christ, and has commissioned us; He has put His seal upon us and given us His Spirit in our hearts as a guarantee.
>
> — 2 Cor 1:21-22

Signed with the perfumed oil by the bishop's hand, the baptized person receives the indelible character, the seal of the Lord, together with the gift of the Spirit, which conforms him more closely to Christ and gives him the grace of spreading the Lord's presence among men.[8]

Growth in the Spirit

As Pentecost follows Easter and is the fruit of the Paschal Mystery, so Confirmation makes Pentecost permanent in the Church and in the lives of its members. The Holy Spirit is God's unrepented gift; one who receives this gift becomes a "temple of the Holy Spirit" (1 Cor 6:19). Even if one strays from the fold, the seal remains, an ever-present invitation to return.

Meanwhile, as the feast of Pentecost brings to completion one part of the liturgical year and dominates the liturgical time that follows it, so does the Spirit rule the lives of those who have received this first of God's gifts. His presence is life, and life is growth. St. Paul describes this growing process as issuing from "the mystery":

> This mystery, which is Christ in you... Him we proclaim, warning every man and teaching every man in all wisdom, that we may present every man mature in Christ.
>
> — Col 1:27-28

Jesus Himself requires growth of us. He compares His teaching to living things — a vine, a seed that produces a crop, a mustard seed that becomes a large plant (cf. Jn 15:1-8; Mk 4:3-20, 31-32; Mt 13:31-32). He astonishes the apostles by cursing a barren fig tree even though it is not the season for figs (cf. Mk 11:5, 20). In His parable of the talents He makes the same point, although in a different way. The man who buries his talent is condemned. "You wicked and slothful servant! You knew that I reap where I have not sowed, and gather where I have not winnowed" (Mt 25:26). "You, therefore," Jesus says to His followers, "must be perfect, as your heavenly Father is perfect" (Mt 5:48). The seal of Confirmation does not let us forget this challenge, this destiny.

To Witness and Defend the Faith

Christ Himself associated the gift of the Holy Spirit and the Christian apostolic mission. "You shall receive power when the Holy Spirit has come upon you; and you shall be my witnesses... to the end of the earth" (Acts 1:8). The Church declares that those who have received this special strength of the Holy Spirit in Confirmation "are more strictly obliged to spread and defend the faith both by word and by deed as true witnesses of Christ" (*LG* 11). The call of the laity to apostolic tasks in the world, and to their role in shaping the kingdom on earth, is related to this sacrament. For the laity, "strengthened by the power of the Holy Spirit through Confirmation, are assigned to the apostolate by the Lord Himself" (*AA* 3).

Growth in the Christian life, precisely because it is a life, cannot be programmed. Here is the difficulty of taking Confirmation as a rite of adult commitment. Grace, indeed, brings about growth. Yet growth also depends on many personal factors, and even perhaps on the experience of spiritual crises, to bring about a realization of what it means to be a child of God and a temple of the Holy Spirit. The grace of Confirmation, though it does not immediately effect such full personal realization, can help to bring it about. The real tragedy is when there is no growth, when the baptized — and perhaps confirmed — live out their Christian vocations in routine mediocrity.

Confirmation and the Paschal Mystery

Confirmation, like all the other sacraments, derives its efficacy from the Paschal Mystery of the Lord's death and resurrection. This is indicated in that "ordinarily Confirmation takes place within Mass."[9] But even if Confirmation is celebrated apart from Mass, its source is still the Paschal Mystery. The chrism, too, signifies the recipient's sharing in this mystery. It recalls the Lord's own anointing (cf. Is 42:1; Mk 1:11).

Yet the chrism also signifies our sharing in the destiny of the Son as the Lord's Anointed, the Messiah. God's revelation of the mysterious Suffering Servant told us something new and startling about the Messiah. Instead of a splendid conqueror, He was to be, and was, "a man of sorrows, and acquainted with grief... despised, and we esteemed Him not" (Is 53:3). As the Master, so the disciple: "Remember the word that I said to you, 'A servant is not greater than his master'" (Jn 15:20).

No Christian can grow to maturity in Christ without accepting His invitation: "If any man would come after Me, let him deny himself and take up his cross daily and follow Me" (Lk 9:23). With St. Paul we must be able to say, "I have been crucified with Christ," if we also wish to say, "It is no longer I who live, but Christ who lives in me" (Gal 2:20). "Take your share of suffering," Paul wrote to Timothy, "as a good soldier of Christ Jesus" (2 Tim 2:3).

The manner of the Holy Spirit's anointing — to inspire and sustain Christians throughout the long Pentecostal season of life — has been told by St. John. The Spirit is the Paraclete, our Advocate, our Counselor.

Isaiah had already told us how the Holy Spirit who dwells in us works through His gifts:

> There shall come forth a shoot from the stump of Jesse, and a branch shall grow out of his roots. And the Spirit of the LORD shall rest upon Him, the spirit of wisdom and understanding, the spirit of counsel and might, the spirit of knowledge and the fear of the LORD.
>
> — Is 11:1-2

Wisdom, understanding, counsel, fortitude, knowledge, piety, and fear of the Lord are commonly known as the gifts of the Holy Spirit.

Finally, the indwelling Spirit will produce in those receptive to His presence what are known as the fruits of the Holy Spirit: love, joy, peace, patience, kindness, generosity, faithfulness, gentleness, faith, modesty, self-control, and chastity (cf. Gal 5:22-23).

Discussion Questions

1. What sacramental graces of Confirmation are continually present in the life of a Christian disciple? What does your sacramental Confirmation mean to you today?

2. Discuss examples of the sacramental graces of Confirmation through which the guidance and strength of the Holy Spirit is given to live the Christian moral life.

3. How are the gifts of the Holy Spirit made real in your daily life? Which of the fruits of the Holy Spirit strengthen your faith and witness to the Gospel?

Additional References:

United States Catholic Catechism for Adults: Chapter 16 — "Confirmation: Consecrated for Mission."

Catechism of the Catholic Church, 1285-1321.

Pope Benedict XVI, *The Sacrament of Charity* (*Sacramentum Caritatis*). Post-Synodal Apostolic Exhortation, February 22, 2007.

Words to Remember...

Confirmation

❑ Confirmation is a sacrament through which we receive the Holy Spirit with His gifts and graces, and thus we are given courage and strength to lead Christian lives.

❑ Confirmation exists to extend to the Church of every time and place the gift of the Holy Spirit sent to the apostles on Pentecost.

❑ Those who have received Confirmation "are more strictly obliged to spread and defend the faith both by word and by deed as true witnesses of Christ" (*LG* 11).

❑ Although any priest can be authorized to administer Confirmation, there is a special propriety in its being conferred by a bishop.

Endnotes to Chapter Five

1. Cf. Pope Pius XII, Encyclical *Mediator Dei* (November 20, 1947), nn. 47-48.

2. *Catechism of the Catholic Church*, 1300.

3. Congregation for Divine Worship, *Rite of Confirmation*, published by authority of Pope Paul VI, August 22, 1971, Introduction, n. 7 (EV 4.1093).

4. Pope Paul VI, Apostolic Constitution *Divinae Consortium Naturae* (August 15, 1971) (EV 4.1067).

5. Cf. St. Thomas Aquinas, *Summa Theologica* III, 65, 1.

6. *Rite of Confirmation*, Introduction, n. 11 (EV 4.1099-1100). The *Code of Canon Law*, canon 891, says that ordinarily it is conferred around the age of discretion but allows for exceptions.

7. *Code of Canon Law*, canon 893.

8. *Rite of Confirmation*, Introduction, n. 9 (EV 4.1096-1097).

9. *Rite of Confirmation*, Introduction, n. 13 (EV 4.1104).

CHAPTER SIX

Sacrament of Healing: Penance and Reconciliation

(*CCC* 1420-1525; 1680-1690)

> Those who approach the sacrament of Penance obtain pardon from the mercy of God for offenses committed against Him, and at the same time are reconciled with the Church, which they have wounded by their sins, and which by charity, example, and prayer seeks their conversion. By the sacred anointing of the sick and the prayer of her priests, the whole Church commends those who are ill to the suffering and glorified Lord, asking that He may lighten their suffering and save them (cf. James 5:14-16).
>
> — *LG* 11

In this chapter we discuss the Sacrament of Penance, one of the sacraments of healing instituted by Christ our Physician.

Gospel Signs

Jesus promulgated the Sacrament of Penance on Easter, thus showing clearly how it arises from the Paschal Mystery of His death and rising:

> On the evening of that day, the first day of the week, the doors being shut where the disciples were, for fear of the Jews, Jesus came and stood among them and said to them, "Peace be with you." When He had said this, He showed them His hands and His side. Then the disciples were glad when they saw the Lord. Jesus said to them again, "Peace be with you. As the Father has sent Me, even so I send you." And when He had said this, He breathed on them, and said to them, "Receive the Holy Spirit.

If you forgive the sins of any, they are forgiven; if you retain the sins of any, they are retained."

— Jn 20:19-23

Thus was the Sacrament of Penance instituted.[1]

... Our Savior, Jesus Christ, when He gave to His apostles and their successors power to forgive sins, instituted in His Church the sacrament of Penance. Thus the faithful who fall into sin after baptism may be reconciled with God and renewed in grace.[2]

Earlier, as is recorded in the Gospel of St. Matthew, Jesus had anticipated this gift. To Peter, who had just professed Him to be the Messiah and who was rewarded by being made the firm foundation of the Church, He said:

"I will give you the keys of the kingdom of heaven, and whatever you bind on earth shall be bound in heaven, and whatever you loose on earth shall be loosed in heaven."

— Mt 16:19

A little later, after the promise to Peter, He extended this power of binding and loosing to "the disciples":

"Truly, I say to you, whatever you bind on earth shall be bound in heaven, and whatever you loose on earth shall be loosed in heaven."

— Mt 18:18

Through the centuries, the Church has exercised this authority to forgive sins. The Sacrament of Penance, the liturgical rite in which the Church does this, has had a variety of forms. But Catholic faith has always believed that Christ continues to forgive sins in His Church.

The Sacramental Sign

The graces of Christ are conferred in the sacraments by means of visible signs — signs that are acts of worship, symbols of the grace conferred, and recognizable gestures through which the Lord confers His gifts. The forgiveness of sins and the restoring of baptismal graces are also attached to an outward sign.

Jesus compared Himself to a physician (cf. Mk 2:17). It was His mission to heal. While He healed bodily ailments, and His human compassion was real, He did not undertake to cure all the human sicknesses. Rather, He used such cures as signs of a more radical moral and spiritual therapy that He desired to extend to all.

> "But that you may know that the Son of man has authority on earth to forgive sins," He said to the paralyzed man, "I say to you, rise, take up your pallet and go home."
>
> — Mk 2:10-11

In this incident the healing of the man's body was a visible sign of forgiveness, but it was not a sacramental sign through which Christ directly conferred grace.

The sign appropriate for the sacrament of forgiveness can be grasped by reflecting on the kind of sickness cured in the Sacrament of Penance. We are concerned now with spiritual illness; and such illness, afflicting an individual in the moral order — that is, in the sphere of his freedom and responsibility — also has social effects. The sign of the physician applying a physical remedy is in the context not altogether adequate. In Penance, two things happen. The sinner is restored with healing grace to share in the divine life, as signified by the young man raised to life at Naim (cf. Lk 7:14), and is welcomed back by the Father, like the prodigal son (cf. Lk 15:20-24). At the same time, the sinner is reinstated in the community and again shares at the community Eucharistic table. God can forgive sins secretly, but it is appropriate for the sinner to be reconciled outwardly, visibly, with the Church community. The community itself is healed as the penitent is healed.

A Saving Tribunal

An analogy for this healing of sickness that affects both the individual and the community is found in the manner society deals with its offenders through a judicial process. The Council of Trent uses this image in developing the theology of Penance and distinguishing this sacrament from Baptism. It explains and justifies this approach by appealing to the power of the keys granted to St. Peter.[3] Moreover, the teaching of Trent, and of the Church today, is that "absolution is given by a priest, who acts as judge."[4] Indeed, in the manner of a merciful judge, the priest — except in the case of penitents in danger of death — ordinarily must have jurisdiction from the local bishop in order to absolve.[5] The *Rite of Penance* states:

> Confession requires in the penitent the will to open his heart to the minister of God, and in the minister a spiritual judgment by which, acting in the person of Christ, He pronounces his decision of forgiveness or retention of sins in accord with the power of the keys.[6]

Jesus Himself was, of course, aware of judges like Pilate, Herod, Caiaphas. He nevertheless took the risk of making a human judicial process the sign of divine justice when He gave to Peter the power of the keys and authorized the apostles to bind and loose on earth (cf. Mt 18:18), just as they would have judicial authority in the age to come (cf. Mt 19:28). Clearly, in his opinion, the sign is not unworthy of a sacrament so necessary and so holy.

The words with which Christ instituted the sacrament ("If you forgive the sins of any...") also contain the authority to judge. It is fitting for the divine tribunal to include dialogue and spiritual counsel. Yet we do not need precisely a sacrament of dialogue or counsel; other available means are adequate for these purposes. As sinners, we need divine forgiveness. Jesus has indicated the sacramental tribunal as his way to forgiveness and reconciliation — a way that in healing the individual sinner also heals the injured community.

Judgment of Mercy

The Sacrament of Penance is an unusual tribunal. The penitent approaches the Lord in sorrow, admitting sin before His representative. The priest, who is Christ's minister in Penance, listens to the confession in the name of the Lord, to discover in the penitent's openness, sorrow, and will to conversion the grounds for a judgment of forgiveness. It is for Christ that the priest hears the confession of guilt; the words spoken to him there are therefore guarded by the most solemn obligation of complete secrecy. It is in the name of Christ that the priest speaks the judgment of the Savior's mercy: "I absolve you from your sins, in the name of the Father, and of the Son, and of the Holy Spirit." Such a sacramental sign is fitting. For Christ, who acts through the sign, is our Judge (cf. Mt 25:31-46). "For we shall all stand before the judgment seat of God" (Rom 14:10).

This form of Penance reminds us also that God's word provides a continuing and merciful judgment throughout our days of pilgrimage. This is shown in the epistle to the Hebrews:

> For the word of God is living and active, sharper than any two-edged sword, piercing to the division of soul and spirit, of joints and marrow, and discerning the thoughts and intentions of the heart. And before Him no creature is hidden, but all are open and laid bare to the eyes of Him with whom we have to do.
>
> — Heb 4:12-13

The continuation of this passage indicates that, for those who live by faith, the judgment is still redemptive, made by the "great high priest who has passed through the heavens" (Heb 4:14).

Similarly, in the Sacrament of Penance, we have, as we move along our pilgrim way, a tribunal of mercy in which judgment is not punitive or final, but healing and redemptive.

Personal Repentance

Sins are not forgiven in any automatic way. In the sacraments, it is Christ who works by His mighty power. Still, as we have seen, the sacraments presuppose (under God's grace) one's quest for God, the core of all religion, expressing itself in a faith that leads to God. They also require, for fruitfulness, a personal response to the grace of God communicated through them. In no sacrament are these personal acts more necessary than in Penance. Very personal inward dispositions are needed in one who comes to Christ for forgiveness.

For full and perfect forgiveness of sins, three acts are required from the penitent as parts of the sacrament. These are contrition, confession, and satisfaction.[7]

Necessity of this Sacrament

For those who have committed mortal sin after baptism, it is necessary to receive this sacrament to recover grace and the friendship of God. A worthy reception of this sacrament is . . .

> . . . the ordinary way of obtaining forgiveness and the remission of serious sins committed after baptism . . . It would therefore be foolish as well as presumptuous . . . to claim to receive forgiveness while doing without the sacrament which was instituted by Christ precisely for forgiveness.[8]

One who repents of a mortal sin but is not able to receive the Sacrament of Penance immediately can receive forgiveness through an act of perfect contrition — that is, sorrow motivated by true love of God — if one is resolved to confess the sin as soon as possible. But those who reject this sacrament of mercy, knowing the gift and the will of Christ that we utilize it, cannot find forgiveness in other ways.

Contrition

Contrition, or sincere sorrow for having offended God, is the most important of the three acts required of the penitent. Contrition is indeed but the other face of love; it is love rejecting all that destroys or threatens it. Hence contrition is placed first, as love must always be given first place (cf. 1 Cor 13:13).

The sinner must come to God by way of repentance. From the beginning of the Gospel, penance is preached as the preparation and condition for entering the kingdom of God. John the Baptist appeared "preaching a baptism of repentance for the forgiveness of sins" (Mk 1:4). This repentance (in Greek, *metanoia*) signifies a complete change of mind, of thinking; it is a turning around, a turning away from sin and a turning toward God. In it we find ourselves again at the heart of the Paschal Mystery, dying in order to live:

For while we live we are always being given up to death for
Jesus' sake, so that the life of Jesus may be manifested in our
mortal flesh.

— 2 Cor 4:11

There can be no forgiveness of sin if we do not have sorrow —
that is, if we do not regret our sin, resolve not to repeat it, and turn
back to God. Sorrow must be interior, from the heart, not merely
expressed on the lips. It must spring from motives of faith, and
not be merely a human sorrow based on regret for some natural bad consequences of our deeds. Sorrow should be supreme:
the conversion to God means putting Him in the first place and
resolving that, aided by His grace, we shall prefer nothing else to
Him. Our sorrow must be universal: we must be sorry for all grave
or mortal sins, sins that exclude one from the friendship of God.

Sorrow for all our sins, even the lesser ones, is urged. Indeed,
it is largely to overcome our venial faults, and so to allow a more
intense faith and charity to rule our lives, that frequent confession
is commended. Certainly one must have sincere sorrow for whatever sins one hopes to have forgiven.

Contrition is called "perfect contrition" if the motive of sorrow is true love for God, if we are sorry because we have offended
the God whom we choose to love above all things. It is called
"perfect" — not because the quality of the penitent's act of contrition is itself perfect, but because charity is the perfect motive
for conversion. Contrition is called "imperfect" if it is based on
some other motive of faith: if, for example, one is sorry because
one believes God, knows God is just and faithful to His word, and
knows one will be rightly punished by God if one does not turn
away from sin to serve him.

Because it is an act of love of God and fruit of God's grace
calling one to repentance, an act of perfect contrition can at once
restore to the friendship of God one who has fallen into serious
sin. But, except in extraordinary circumstances, one who has separated from Christ and the family of faith by grave sin is seriously
obliged to receive the Sacrament of Penance before receiving the
Eucharist. One who has a grave need to communicate and has no

chance to go to confession is obliged to make a perfect act of contrition, which includes a promise to confess as soon as possible.[9]

Sorrow for sin implies a resolve not to fall back into sin. While we cannot be certain that our frailty will not betray us again, our present resolve must be honest and realistic. We must will to change, to be faithful to our Lord, to take realistic steps to make faithfulness possible. Christ's forgiveness always called for this. "Go, and do not sin again" (Jn 8:11).

Confession

The words of Christ instituting the Sacrament of Penance suggest that the minister of His forgiveness is to discriminate wisely: "If you forgive the sins of any..." The Church teaches[10] that it is necessary by divine law to confess to a priest each and every mortal sin — and also circumstances which make a sin a more serious kind of mortal sin — that one can remember after a careful examination of conscience. Sins committed before baptism do not have to be confessed, for in baptism all sins of the past are forgiven. Moreover, a mortal sin which has been once confessed and for which absolution has been received need not be confessed again.

Devout penitents frequently are guilty of no grave sins; but they may fruitfully bring before Christ with sorrow the venial sins that mar their lives and limit their charity, taking care to have true sorrow for the sins they do confess. It is not necessary to seek to remember and to confess all the imperfections in one's life. Confessions of devotion may profitably center on those faults for which one can and should have a more genuine sorrow, because of the harm they do to others, or because of the way in which they hinder one's progress in grace.

Satisfaction

The Church believes that there are "temporal punishments" for sin. This means that the just and merciful God requires that the penitent sinner atone for his sins; he will receive punishment for them either in this life or after death in purgatory, unless he has taken punishment upon himself by deeds of penance.

That there are temporal punishments for sin is evidenced throughout the long history of Israel in all that it suffered for its infidelities, especially in its captivity. The sins of individuals have similar consequences. Moses is forgiven his doubt, but because of it he is not permitted to enter the Promised Land. David is forgiven his adultery, but the desired child of the sinful union does not survive. Temporal punishment persists even in death. Thus, we read in the Second Book of Maccabees of the value of praying for the dead (cf. 2 Macc 12:43-46). St. Paul also indicates there is purification beyond death (cf. 1 Cor 3:10-15).

Penitents, then, must complete their penitential acts by making some satisfaction for their sins, by doing a "penance" imposed by the priest. The penance imposed in earlier days was often severe. Today, the penance is usually the recitation of certain prayers assigned by the priest to the penitent.

> The kind and extent of the satisfaction should be suited to the personal condition of each penitent so that each one may restore the order which he disturbed and through the corresponding remedy be cured of the sickness from which he suffered. Therefore, it is necessary that the act of Penance really be a remedy for sin and a help to renewal of life.[11]

Our sins are more serious than we realize, and our deeds of penance are often slight. To assist us in our frailty, the Church also makes possible indulgences for the faithful. An indulgence is a remission before God of all (plenary indulgence) or part (partial indulgence) of the temporal punishment due to sins that have already been forgiven.[12]

The principle underlying indulgences is as old as the Church. It is based on the doctrine of the Mystical Body of Christ. All members of this Body, St. Paul wrote (cf. 1 Cor 12:21-26), should contribute to the well-being of an ailing member. Fully aware of the infinite and decisive value of Christ's atoning death, Paul rejoiced that his own sufferings could benefit the Christians of Colossae, and he added:

In my flesh I complete what is lacking in Christ's afflictions for the sake of His body, that is, the church.

— Col 1:24

The Church teaches that in virtue of the authority given it by Christ, it may grant to sinners who have already received forgiveness of their sins a share in the merits of Christ and the saints, so that the burden of temporal punishment due for sins may be removed or lightened.

To gain an indulgence, one must say the prayer or do the good deed to which the Church attaches the indulgence, be in the state of grace, and have the proper intention. By a kind of spiritual leverage, as it were, a relatively slight act of piety on the part of the individual brings upon him a great mercy.[13]

The "Laborious Baptism"

The Council of Trent, citing St. Gregory of Nazianzus and St. John of Damascus, stated that the Sacrament of Penance "has rightly been called by the holy Fathers 'a laborious kind of baptism.'"[14] In the same place the Council of Trent also asserted — against certain teachings of the day — that it is a sacrament distinct from Baptism. It is called "a kind of baptism" because it restores baptismal holiness, and "laborious" because it cannot do this "without many tears and labors on our part."

Penance does really restore or renew baptismal holiness. When this holiness has been lost, it can be recovered in the sacrament of Penance. A Catholic who has committed grave sin is obliged to ask forgiveness for it in this sacrament. One should do so promptly. Church law requires confession of sins once a year; though, strictly speaking, this particular law does not bind those who would have no grave sins to confess.[15]

But Penance is also useful to renew baptismal innocence — that is, to return it to full splendor — even when there are only venial sins or faults committed amidst the moral struggles of everyday living. In fact . . .

Frequent and careful celebration of this sacrament is also very useful as a remedy for venial sins. This is not a mere ritual repetition or psychological exercise, but a serious striving to perfect the grace of baptism so that, as we bear in our body the death of Jesus Christ, His life may be seen in us ever more clearly.[16]

Penance and Children

The idea of a "laborious baptism" for children suggests a practical program to prepare them for the Sacrament of Penance. When infants are baptized, parents and sponsors act for them. As the minds of children develop, however, they can learn the meaning of baptism and also prepare for the second "laborious baptism." They can act out and relive their own infant baptism as they prepare to receive the Sacrament of Penance.

A child's introduction to the Sacrament of Penance is not to be long delayed, for while the capacity to reason is evolving gradually in a child, his moral conscience too is being trained —that is, the faculty of judging his acts in relation to a norm of morality. An early introduction to Penance will help the child make personal the choice implicit in his baptism. That baptism was a conversion, a turning to Christ; the first confession can be an early help in making that basic conversion more personal and free. Church law requires that the practice of having children receive the sacrament of Penance before First Communion be maintained.[17]

The suitable age for the first reception of these sacraments (Penance and the Eucharist) is deemed to be that which in documents of the Church is called the "age of reason" or of "discretion." This age, for both Confession and Communion, is that at which the child begins to reason — that is, about the seventh year, more or less. From that time on, the obligation of fulfilling the precepts of Confession and Communion begins.[18]

The Community Dimension

Viewing the Sacrament of Penance as a second baptism enables us also to realize that it is, indeed, part of the public liturgy of the Church. As Baptism in the first place incorporates us into the Body of Christ, so Penance restores to life within that Body one who by grave sin had ceased to be a living member. A public ritual of reconciliation made this clear in the early Church. Today, in approaching Penance anew as reconciliation with the community as well as with God, and perhaps within a communal service, the parallel with Baptism offers a perspective for seeing Penance as belonging to the liturgical celebration of the whole Church community.

As Pope Benedict XVI notes:

> The relationship between the Eucharist and the sacrament of Reconciliation reminds us that sin is never a purely individual affair; it always damages the ecclesial communion that we have entered through Baptism.
>
> — *Sacramentum Caritatis*, 20

Communal Penance

The Second Vatican Council decreed:

> The rite and formulas for the sacrament of Penance are to be revised so that they may more clearly express the nature and effect of the sacrament.
>
> — *SC* 72

Penance thus could not remain unaffected by the fundamental change of the whole modern liturgical reform, namely, the growing sense of community as God's covenanted people, every member of which is invited to enter fully into His worship. Moreover, since Penance was a community celebration among the early Christians, there was already at hand a model for reforming this rite, which in modern times had become relatively isolated from community celebration. What was needed, therefore — and what gradually came about — was the restoration of Penance as a communal celebration in the Church.

To show more clearly that Penance is a genuine liturgical celebration, it may be celebrated as an act of community worship, which forms the context of private confession. This was the practice of the early Church. While certain classes of sins were confessed privately to the bishop, and in time to a priest, this was done within a public liturgy that was carried out during Lent. This paralleled and widened the liturgy of resurrection, centered in the first place on the catechumens.

Something more is needed, however, if there is to be a genuinely communal Penance liturgy. There must also be a sense of the communal and ecclesial dimension of sin. In the early Church, sinners guilty of some grave sins were excommunicated, required to do public works of penance, and were reconciled to God through the Church on Holy Thursday by returning to the Eucharist. Even in private confession there is a residue of this public penance. Penitents publicly join the line of people waiting to confess. Meanwhile they must, if guilty of grave sin, exclude themselves from Communion until they return to the life of grace within the Church through the Sacrament of Penance. Their reconciliation with God and community is completed when they return publicly to the Eucharistic table.

To acknowledge — even to become aware — that our sins have a community dimension is not always easy, and perhaps not very pleasant for many in an era marked by highly individualistic thinking. By public penance we do not escape personal responsibility; we, in fact, enlarge the area of our awareness of responsibility for the sins of the society of which we are a part.

Since we are all members of one body in Christ, the sickness of one member causes a malaise throughout the body. At the very least, the failures of individuals hinder the growth and restrict the vitality of the whole body.

> If one member suffers, all suffer together; if one member is honored, all rejoice together.
>
> —1 Cor 12:26

> By the hidden and loving mystery of God's design men are joined together in the bonds of supernatural solidarity, so much so that the sin of one harms the others just as the holiness of one benefits the others.[19]

Social Dimensions of Sin

Within this wider context, all particular sins except those directly against God, such as blasphemy, are offenses against God's law precisely because they injure one's neighbor or oneself. But even those which directly harm only oneself have a potential for disturbing community harmony. The last seven commandments of the Decalogue are concerned with our neighbor. If I steal, for example, I injure my neighbor and perhaps cause privation to my neighbor's family. I also lower the level of openness and mutual confidence in the whole community, and in a sense I diminish the pulse and flow of life in the Body of Christ. This is true even of "secret" sins against the ninth and tenth commandments, which also have reference to my neighbor. Even blasphemy and other sins against the first three commandments can cause scandal. In a word, my personal and even secret sins can have extensive consequences in the community.

Moreover, certain evils involving personal guilt, especially sins of omission, have a communal dimension. An example here is racism. As a web that enmeshes all, it involves us all in its consequences.

The same is true of all widespread social injustices. Although few of us may be involved in large and dramatic ways, a very great many of us are in some measure responsible.

> Countless millions are starving, countless families are destitute, countless men are steeped in ignorance; countless people need schools, hospitals, and homes worthy of the name. In such circumstances, we cannot tolerate public and private expenditures of a wasteful nature; we cannot approve a debilitating arms race.... No one is permitted to disregard the plight of his brothers living in dire poverty, enmeshed in ignorance and tormented by insecurity. The Christian, moved by this sad state of affairs, should echo the words of Christ: "I have compassion on the crowd" (Mk 8:2).[20]

In 1971, the synod of bishops spoke of the "serious injustices which are building around the world of men a network of domination, oppression, and abuses which stifle freedom and which keep the greater part of humanity from sharing in the building up and enjoyment of a more just and fraternal world"; the world is marked by a "grave sin of injustice."[21]

The follower of Christ will consider his social responsibilities and the social dimensions of sin in his examination of conscience.[22]

Celebrating the Sacrament

The Sacrament of Penance may be administered in two ways, either within a communal ceremony or in an individual one. Even the communal ceremony guards important personal elements of the sacrament: the individual penitent confesses his sins in private and there is individual absolution. And even the individual form guards certain public elements, as an act of the Church's liturgy must. The sacrament is usually administered in a publicly recognized place; a penitent who has sinned gravely must refrain from sharing in the Eucharistic table until he has been absolved; the priest who administers the sacrament must, except in special cases of necessity, be one who has been given public authority to absolve by the bishop of the place.

The Ancient Practice

The early Christians also confessed their sins privately, although within a community celebration. The real difference between ancient and modern practice, however, is that some early Christians felt they could receive the Sacrament of Penance only once, and it was only with difficulty that they came to feel Penance could be received more often. The early Christians had such an exalted idea of the holiness befitting the baptized that it was hard for them to entertain the idea of a Christian relapsing into serious sin, at least repeatedly. There developed a tendency to defer absolution until the approach of death.

The Celtic monks broke through this difficulty by making private and frequent confession popular — first in their monasteries, then outside, and finally in their missionary journeys to the Continent, as Europe strove to recover from the barbarian invasions. For the tortured in conscience, Penance became a sacrament not only of healing but of continuing mercy. For the devout, it became a means of deepening their conversion and promoting their growth in the Spirit. In this spirit, the Church recommends regular and frequent confession. It summons those in grave sin to prompt repentance. It urges the devout through use of the sacraments to receive the healing and sanctifying gifts of Christ.

The Rite of Penance

The *Rite of Penance* joins ancient and modern practice in a ceremony of reconciliation. Private administration of the sacrament, while retaining its judicial character, also continues to offer its merciful healing. It may do this within the setting of a communal service. "Communal celebration shows more clearly the ecclesial nature of Penance."[23] Such celebrations acknowledge the social dimension of sin and the need to be reconciled to the community as one returns to God. The faithful support one another in their participation in communal celebration of Penance. The readings, hymns, and prayers of the ceremony bind them together as a family of God, coming before Him in sorrow and assisting each penitent to deeper personal repentance and new resolve.

The individual ceremony also has certain advantages. It retains certain features of public worship, as noted above. The ceremonies suggested for it — such as the reading of a scriptural passage by the priest or by the penitent, and the priest's extension of his hands over the head of the penitent while saying the words of absolution — can add even more dignity to its celebration. The individual ceremony has considerable flexibility, providing an opportunity for combining a spiritual direction and pastoral guidance with the administration of the sacrament. Yet it is also an ecclesial act, a reconciliation with the Christian community, as the introduction to the words of absolution make clear:

> God, the Father of mercies,
> through the death and resurrection of His Son
> has reconciled the world to Himself
> and sent the Holy Spirit among us for the forgiveness of sins:
> through the ministry of the Church may God give you pardon and peace,
> and I absolve you...[24]

When for extraordinary reasons groups of people are not able to confess their sins individually, they may in some circumstances receive sacramental forgiveness by a communal absolution. Such communal absolution, however, may be given only when there is a "grave need," which is to be determined by the local bishop, "who is to consult with the other members of the episcopal conference." [25] Unless prevented by some good reason, those who receive communal absolution should go to confession before receiving communal absolution again. [26] Unless it is morally impossible for them to do so, they are obliged to go to confession within a year.

> Individual, integral confession and absolution remain the only ordinary way for the faithful to reconcile themselves with God and the Church, unless physical or moral impossibility excuses from this kind of confession. [27]

Whether the Sacrament of Penance is administered in individual ceremony or within a communal celebration, the deepest joy of the guilty is in their deliverance from the sin in a new Passover that frees them from the grossest kind of servitude. They come forth from the sacrament, their turning to God complete, in the gladness of a clear conscience and restored justice, with the exhilarating prospect of a fresh start. Once more they are a "new creation"; once more for them, "the new has come" (2 Cor 5:17).

--------------------- **Discussion Questions** ---------------------

1. Why is the Sacrament of Penance and Reconciliation offered to us after Baptism?
2. Discuss the example of one sinner turned saint, such as St. Augustine. How does the life of the saint show God's unconditional, forgiving love made sacramentally present in Penance and Reconciliation?
3. Why confess our sins to a priest? (*CCC* 1461-1467) Discuss reasons why participation in this sacrament is important for ongoing conversion and growth in the Christian life.

Additional References:

United States Catholic Catechism for Adults: Chapter 18 — "Sacrament of Penance and Reconciliation: God Is Rich in Mercy." *Catechism of the Catholic Church*, 1420-1525.

Pope Benedict XVI, *The Sacrament of Charity* (*Sacramentum Caritatis*). Post-Synodal Apostolic Exhortation, February 22, 2007.

Words to Remember...

Penance

❑ Christ gave us the Sacrament of Penance on Easter, the day He rose from the dead.

❑ Those going to confession must have a true sorrow for their sins and a purpose of amendment; they must confess their sins, especially all mortal sins that have not previously been forgiven; and they must resolve to perform the penance assigned.

❑ Christians who have committed grave sins have a serious duty to receive the Sacrament of Penance; those who have committed only lesser sins can also profit greatly from this sacrament.

Endnotes to Chapter Six

1. Cf. Council of Trent, Session 14, November 25, 1551, *Doctrine on the Sacrament of Penance*, ch. 1 (DS 1670), and canon 3 on the Sacrament of Penance (DS 1703).

2. Congregation for Divine Worship, *Rite of Penance*, published by authority of Pope Paul VI (December 2, 1973), Introduction, n. 2 (EV 4.2677).

3. Cf. Council of Trent, Session 14, November 25, 1551, *Doctrine on Sacrament of Penance*, chs. 2 (DS 1671) and 5 (DS 1679).

4. Congregation for the Doctrine of the Faith, *Sacramentum Paenitentiae* ("Pastoral Norms concerning the Administration of General Sacramental Absolution," June 16, 1972) (EV 4.1653). Cf. Council of Trent, Session 14, November 25, 1551, *Doctrine on the Sacrament of Penance*, ch. 6 (DS 1685), and canon 9 on the Sacrament of Penance (DS 1709).

5. Cf., e.g., *Rite of Penance*, Introduction, n. 9b (EV 4.2690); *Code of Canon Law*, canon 969.

6. *Rite of Penance*, Introduction, n. 6b (EV 4.2683).

7. Cf. *Rite of Penance*, Introduction, n. 6 (EV 4.2681-2684). Cf. Council of Trent, Session 14, November 25, 1551, *Doctrine on the Sacrament of Penance*, ch. 3 (DS 1673), and canon 4 on the Sacrament of Penance (DS 1704); Congregation for the Doctrine of Faith, *Sacramentum Paenitentiae* ("Pastoral Norms concerning the Administration of General Sacramental Absolution," June 16, 1972) (EV 4.1653-1667).

8. Pope John Paul II, Post-Synodal Apostolic Exhortation *Reconciliatio et Paenitentia* (December 2, 1984), n. 31 (EV 9.1181).

9. Cf. *Code of Canon Law*, canon 916; Council of Trent, Session 13, October 11, 1551, *Decree on the Most Holy Eucharist*, ch. 7 (DS 1647).

10. Cf. *Rite of Penance*, Introduction, n. 7a (EV 4.2687); Council of Trent, Session 14, Nov. 25, 1551, *Doctrine on the Sacrament of Penance*, canon 7 on the Sacrament of Penance (DS 1707); Congregation for the Doctrine of the Faith, *Sacramentum Paenitentiae* ("Pastoral Norms concerning the Administration of General Sacramental Absolution," June 16, 1972) (EV 4.1653-1667). Cf. also *Code of Canon Law*, canon 988.1.

11. *Rite of Penance*, Introduction, n. 6c (EV 4.2684).

12. Cf. Pope Paul VI, Apostolic Constitution *Indulgentiarum Doctrina* (January 1, 1967), Norm 1 (EV 2.935). This document, also on pp. 85-118 in *Enchirdion Indulgentiarum* (Libreria Editrice Vaticana, 1986), explains the history and theology of indulgences fairly fully. Cf. also Council of Trent, Session 25, December 4, 1563, *Decree on Indulgences* (DS 1835).

13. Cf. *Code of Canon Law*, canon 996.

14. Council of Trent, Session 14, November 25, 1551, *Doctrine on the Sacrament of Penance*, ch. 2 (DS 1672). Cf. St. Gregory of Nazianzus, *Oratio* 39.17 (MG 36.356); St. John of Damascus, *De Fide Orthodoxa* 4.9 (MG 94.1124).

15. Cf. *Code of Canon Law*, canon 989.

16. *Rite of Penance*, Introduction, n. 7b (EV 4.2687).

17. Cf. Congregation for the Clergy, *General Directory for Catechesis* (August 11, 1997), nos. 177-181 (EV 16.608-1011).

18. Cf. Congregation for the Sacraments, *Quam Singulari* (August 8, 1910), and frequently otherwise.

19. *Rite of Penance*, Introduction, n. 5 (EV 4.2680).

20. Pope Paul VI, Encyclical *Progressio Populorum* (March 26, 1967), nn. 53, 74 (EV 2.1098-1119).

21. Second General Assembly of the Synod of Bishops, 1971, *Justice in the World*, Introduction and Part II (EV 4.1238-1243, 1264-1273).

22. Cf. the outline examination of conscience in *Rite of Penance*, Appendix III.

23. *Rite of Penance*, Introduction, n. 22 (EV 4.2703).

24. *Rite of Penance*, n. 46.

25. Cf. *Rite of Penance*, Introduction, nn. 31-33 (EV 4.2712-2715). Cf. *Code of Canon Law*, canon 961.

26. Cf. *Rite of Penance*, Introduction, n. 34 (EV 4.2716). Cf. also *Code of Canon Law*, canon 962.1.

27. *Rite of Penance*, Introduction, n. 31 (EV 4.2712).

CHAPTER SEVEN

The Sacrament of the Anointing of the Sick

(CCC 1499-1532)

Christ and the Infirm

Our Lord had compassion on the sick. He revealed Himself to John as the Messiah simply by saying:

> "The blind receive their sight and the lame walk, lepers are cleansed and the deaf hear, and the dead are raised up, and the poor have good news preached to them."
>
> — Mt 11:5

In the parable of the great banquet, the servants were commanded, "Go out quickly to the streets and lanes of the city, and bring in the poor and maimed and blind and lame" (Lk 14:21). Many of His works were cures of the sick; and we have seen in the preceding section how He Himself, as well as the evangelists, deliberately used these works as signs of a spiritual healing (cf. Mk 2:10-11).

Anointing in Scripture

Jesus not only taught His disciples to be compassionate, but He also told them who should be the special objects of their compassion. The parable of the great banquet with its humble guests was preceded by an instruction that He gave at a banquet: "But when you give a banquet, invite the poor, the crippled, the lame, and the blind" (Lk 14:13). In His parable previewing the Last Judgment, those were punished to whom He said, "I was sick and you did not visit me..." (Mt 25:43). On the other hand, they were rewarded to whom He said, "I was sick and you visited me..." (Mt 25:36).

Meanwhile, the apostles assisted Him in His mission:

> He called to Him His twelve disciples and gave them author-
> ity over unclean spirits, to cast them out, and to heal every
> disease and every infirmity.
>
> — Mt 10:1

A similar commission was given to them after the Resurrection:

> "They will lay their hands on the sick, and they will recover."
>
> — Mk 16:18

In an earlier passage in the Gospel of St. Mark, we read:

> And they cast out many demons, and anointed with oil many
> that were sick and healed them.
>
> — Mk 6:13

This is the first allusion to the Sacrament of the Anointing of
the Sick.[1] Jesus here authorized a practice that may have already
existed in exorcistic healings, but He gave it a new meaning. Like
His own healings, those of His disciples were signs proclaiming
the coming of the kingdom:

> "The Spirit of the Lord is upon me, because He has anointed
> me to preach good news to the poor. He has sent me to pro-
> claim release to the captives and recovering of sight to the
> blind, to set at liberty those who are oppressed, to proclaim
> the acceptable year of the Lord."
>
> — Lk 4:18-19; cf. Isa. 61:1-2

In His Church, Christ wished all to care for the sick. The
ministry to the sick is an obligation of every Christian. In a special
way, however, Christ charged His priests to anoint the sick while
praying over them in a sacramental gesture that would be more
properly a deed of His own personal care (cf. Jas 5:14).

As with the Sacrament of Confirmation, we first see the actual
anointing of the sick in the early Church described in the epistle
of St. James. The letter is chiefly a moral exhortation, and it is
only as part of such an exhortation that the sacrament is spoken
of. Thus:

> Is any one among you suffering? Let him pray. Is any cheerful? Let him sing praise.
>
> — Jas 5:13

Then:

> Is any among you sick? Let him call for the elders of the church, and let them pray over him, anointing him with oil in the name of the Lord; and the prayer of faith will save the sick man, and the Lord will raise him up; and if he has committed sins, he will be forgiven.
>
> — Jas 5:14-15

This passage is cited by the Council of Trent when it declares:

> This sacred anointing of the sick was instituted by Christ our Lord as truly and properly a sacrament of the New Testament.[2]

Sacrament of the Sick

The Sacrament of Anointing of the Sick is — as the words of St. James make clear — for the sick and infirm.

Accordingly, "There should be special care and concern that those who are dangerously ill due to sickness or old age receive this sacrament."[3] Relatives and friends of the sick have a responsibility in charity to assist them in calling the priest, or to help get them ready to receive the sacrament worthily, especially in the case of graver illnesses.

During some centuries, there was a tendency to reserve this sacrament only for those quite near death; thus, the sacrament came to be called "Extreme Unction" — that is, "Last Anointing." However, the Church has made it clear that it wishes this sacrament for the sick to be more generously available.

> "Extreme unction," which may also more fittingly be called "anointing of the sick," is not a sacrament for those only who are at the point of death. Hence, as soon as any one of the faithful begins to be in danger of death from sickness or old age, the appropriate time for him to receive this sacrament has certainly already arrived.
>
> — SC 73

Thus, there is no need to wait until a person is at the point of death. Determining whether there is a dangerous illness is simply a matter of prudent judgment; there is no need for scrupulosity.[4] "The sacrament may be repeated if the sick person recovers after anointing or if, during the same illness, the danger becomes more serious."[5] Moreover, "a sick person should be anointed before surgery when a dangerous illness is the reason for the surgery."[6]

The Church further teaches:

Old people may be anointed if they are in weak condition even though no dangerous illness is present. Sick children may be anointed if they have sufficient use of reason to be comforted by this sacrament.

Also, the faithful "should be encouraged to ask for the anointing and, as soon as the time for the anointing comes, to receive it with faith and devotion, not misusing this sacrament by putting it off." People who are unconscious or who have lost the use of reason may be anointed "if, as Christian believers, they would have asked for it were they in control of their faculties." However, a priest is not to anoint "a person already dead." If there is a doubt as to death, the priest may administer the sacrament conditionally.[7]

The Sacrament of Anointing of the Sick extends the healing hand of Christ; it is an encounter with Christ the Healer, Christ the divine Physician. The woman in the Gospel was eager to touch only the Lord's cloak: "If I touch even His garments," she thought, "I shall be made well" (Mk 5:28). The sick person today "touches" Christ and experiences His power through the sacramental anointing.

The Community Dimension

Sickness is a crisis of life, both for the individuals who are ill and for the communities to which they belong. Even pagan societies have understood this and provided some socioreligious ritual to help resolve the crisis. St. James clearly sees the community dimension of sickness when he says that the sick person should "call for the elders of the church." These "elders" — that is, "presbyters" —

represent the community and the community's concern. Such concern is further shown in the "prayer of faith" that St. James says will reclaim the one who is ill; the prayer arises from the community of faith, the Church gathered around the sick person precisely to invoke "the name of the Lord."

The *Rite of Anointing and Pastoral Care of the Sick* provides a substantial and expressive liturgy. It begins with a greeting, introduction, and penitential rite (which may be replaced by sacramental Penance). A Liturgy of the Word follows. Suitable readings are suggested. Friends and relatives can add a communal dimension; they may assist in the readings, as also in prayers and singing. There may be a homily, after which the sacrament is conferred.

First, there is a laying on of hands — that characteristic scriptural gesture of blessing — by all the priests who are participating. Then, the minister of the sacrament anoints the recipient's forehead and hands — or, in case of necessity, the forehead only or another part of the body. This anointing is also a laying on of hands, now with the blessed oil.

The sacramental sign is especially this anointing, together with the prayer that accompanies it:

Through this holy anointing
may the Lord in His love and mercy help you
with the grace of the Holy Spirit.
(Amen.)
May the Lord who frees you from sin
save you and raise you up.
(Amen.)[8]

This prayer speaks of salvation and resurrection with the wise ambiguity of St. James, and it treats the sacrament as the gift of the Holy Spirit, who is also God's first gift to the Church through the Paschal Mystery.

The oil used for the anointing is olive oil, although the use of another oil may be authorized if olive oil is not available. Ordinarily, the oil is blessed by the bishop at the Chrism Mass on Holy Thursday, a custom that also recalls how this sacrament derives its power from the Paschal Mystery. Oil signifies strength and health.

In the blessing, the bishop prays that "all anointed with this oil ... may be freed from pain, illness, and disease and made well again in body, mind, and soul." By an invocation taken from the earliest known blessing for the oil of the sick, he further begs that God will "send the Holy Spirit, the Comforter, from heaven upon this oil which nature has provided." Even in sickness, therefore, the Holy Spirit, the gift of the Paschal Mystery, continues His care.

The ceremony of anointing of the sick concludes with a special prayer for the sick, followed by the Lord's Prayer, perhaps the reception of Communion, and a blessing.

The anointing may also be done within the Mass. This indicates the source of the sacrament, the mystery of the Lord's death and resurrection, continued in the Mass and the origin of all sacramental power. This mystery also gives meaning to human suffering, as we shall see, and draws it, with the Passion of the Lord, into resurrection.

The Sacramental Grace

The fruit of this sacrament is indicated in these words of St. James:

> ... and the prayer of faith will save the sick man, and the Lord will raise him up.
>
> — Jas 5:15

The ambiguity here is simply the result of the way biblical people look at sickness, as distinct from our modern way. They see it not merely as a physical reality but as situated in actual condition of sin. Further, they do not distinguish clearly between body and soul, but see the individual as a unity; the healing is intended for the whole person.

Pope Paul VI, quoting the Council of Trent, explains and summarizes the effects of the sacrament:

> This reality is in fact the grace of the Holy Spirit, whose anointing takes away sins, if any still remain to be taken away, and the remnants of sin; it also relieves and strengthens the soul of the sick person, arousing in him a great confidence in the divine mercy; thus sustained, he may easily bear the trials

and hardships of his sickness, more easily resist the temptations of the devil "lying in wait" (cf. Gen 3:15), and sometimes regain bodily health, if this is expedient for the health of the soul.[9]

The Anointing of the Sick is not intended to replace the Sacrament of Penance. The Sacrament of Penance should precede the anointing,[10] and it would be gravely wrong to receive the sacrament of Anointing of the Sick while one is knowingly guilty of grave sin. Still, in certain circumstances, the Anointing of the Sick may replace Penance. If the person to be anointed is unconscious and in grave sin, but is prepared by prior acts of faith and hope and right fear of God so that he is properly disposed to receive the gifts of a sacrament, the Sacrament of Anointing of the Sick brings forgiveness of even serious sin.

The sacrament draws those who receive it into that interior penance, that *metanoia*, which leads into the mystery of Christ. That such a sacrament has been instituted shows also that suffering does not of itself bring salvation; if our suffering is to be a means of healing, the Lord Himself must associate it with His death and resurrection. As St. James indicates, that is the distinctive sacramental grace of the Anointing of the Sick.

This sacrament "prolongs the concern which the Lord Himself showed in the bodily and spiritual welfare of the sick, as the gospels testify, and which He asked His followers to show also."[11] It "provides the sick person with the grace of the Holy Spirit, by which the whole man is brought to health, trust in God is encouraged, and strength is given to resist the temptations of the Evil One and anxiety about death."[12]

The sacramental action of Christ on the whole person, body and soul, while it may lead to physical healing, goes beyond this to mental and spiritual health and even to eternal salvation:

> The sick man will be saved by his faith and the faith of the Church which looks back to the death and resurrection of Christ, the source of the sacrament's power, and looks ahead to the future kingdom which is pledged in the sacraments.[13]

Sickness and the Paschal Mystery

The Second Vatican Council, in speaking of the Anointing of the Sick, showed how sufferings caused by sickness may be drawn into the Paschal Mystery. The whole Church, said the council, exhorts the sick "to contribute to the welfare of the People of God by associating themselves freely with the passion and death of Christ" (*LG* 11). The council cited in illustration certain passages of the New Testament:

> We are children of God, and if children, then heirs, heirs of God and fellow heirs with Christ, provided we suffer with Him in order that we may also be glorified with Him.
>
> — Rom 8:16-17

> Now I rejoice in my sufferings for your sake, and in my flesh I complete what is lacking in Christ's afflictions for the sake of His body, that is, the church.
>
> — Col 1:24

> The saying is sure: If we have died with Him, we shall also live with Him; if we endure, we shall also reign with Him.
>
> — 2 Tim 2:11-12

> But rejoice in so far as you share Christ's sufferings, that you may also rejoice and be glad when His glory is revealed.
>
> — 1 Pet 4:13

Anointing of the sick, whether or not it heals the body, becomes a remedy for the spirit in which all events are drawn together in a hopeful and joyous experience of life even in its hardships.

> So we do not lose heart. Though our outer nature is wasting away, our inner nature is being renewed every day. For this slight momentary affliction is preparing for us an eternal weight of glory beyond all comparison, because we look not to the things that are seen but to the things that are unseen; for the things that are seen are transient, but the things that are unseen are eternal.
>
> — 2 Cor 4:16-18

St. James says all this when he attributes the healing to the Lord, in whose name the prayer of faith is uttered. In all their weakness and in all their trust, the sick encounter the healing power of the Lord's death and resurrection in this sacrament. The Lord "will save the sick man" and "raise him up" (Jas 5:15).

The Sacrament of the Dying

Eventually, all physical remedies fail. In the cycle of life in a person's present condition, life begins, grows, matures, declines, and ends in death. Although anointing should be given at the onset of dangerous illness or in the weakness of old age, the Church allows the sacrament to be administered again if there has been a recovery and relapse, or if the danger becomes more serious. If the sickness continues or deepens, the invalid may and should receive the Eucharist regularly.

Communion received by the dying is called Viaticum, "food for the journey" — here, the spiritual food one takes for his last journey.

> When the Christian, in his passage from this life, is strengthened by the body and blood of Christ, he has the pledge of the resurrection which the Lord promised: "He who feeds on my flesh and drinks my blood has life eternal, and I will raise him up on the last day" (Jn 6:54). Viaticum should be received during Mass when possible so that the sick person may receive communion under both kinds. Communion received as Viaticum should be considered a special sign of participation in the mystery of the death of the Lord and his passage to the Father, the mystery which is celebrated in the Eucharist.[14]

In death, sign gives way to Reality; but on the journey the Eucharistic sign containing Reality is the most appropriate provision, which is the very meaning of the word *Viaticum*. Soon, however, the bonds of the sign will burst, and Reality will be seen "face to face" (1 Cor 13:12).

Even "death is swallowed up in victory" (1 Cor 15:54), and only in death does the Christian retrieve all past losses and reap a hundredfold and receive everlasting life (cf. Mt 19:29). The ordeal of sickness, losses and privations through various trials, and accumulating diminishments of aging, are so many little deaths — mystical deaths, as writers have called them, losses foreshadowing the final separation through death from all that is here loved. Yet in this final and complete loss, all is retrieved. "He who sows bountifully will reap bountifully" (2 Cor 9:6).

Catholic Funerals

The funeral of the Christian recalls the words of Christ concerning the seed: "But if it dies, it bears much fruit" (Jn 12:24). In every Eucharist, we say, "We wait in joyful hope for the coming of our Savior, Jesus Christ." Those who have died have passed beyond the sacramental care of the Church. If they have died in grace, even if they need a final purification in purgatory, they are secure, "at home with the Lord" (2 Cor 5:8).

Still, the Church does not forget them, for they remain one with us in the Communion of Saints.

> Even dead, we are not at all separated from one another, because we all run the same course and we will find one another again in the same place. We shall never be separated... we shall all be together in Christ.[15]

Some forms of funerals are simple. But in the most desirable funeral rite, the Eucharistic sacrifice is the heart of the celebration of our sorrow, our hope, and our faith. There, Christ's death and resurrection are made present to us. Those who have loved the deceased may receive the Lord, in whom we are all one and in whom we all live, the Lord who for each of us is "the resurrection and the life" (Jn 11:25).

——————————— Discussion Questions ———————————

1. Discuss the concrete ways in which the Sacrament of the Anointing of the Sick and the Dying continues the healing ministry of Jesus in the Gospels.

2. Discuss the relationship of the Sacrament of Baptism to the Sacrament of the Anointing of the Sick and the Dying.
3. Reflect on the *Rite of Anointing and Pastoral Care of the Sick* and the sacramental meaning of each ritual action.

Additional References:

United States Catholic Catechism for Adults: Chapter 19 — "Anointing the Sick and the Dying."

Catechism of the Catholic Church, 1499-1532.

Pope Benedict XVI, *The Sacrament of Charity* (*Sacramentum Caritatis*). Post-Synodal Apostolic Exhortation, February 22, 2007.

Words to Remember...

Anointing of the Sick

❑ Christ instituted the Anointing of the Sick to comfort the sick and the dying, and to assist them spiritually and bodily.

❑ Only priests and bishops can confer this Anointing of the Sick, using oil blessed for this purpose.

❑ The time to anoint the sick has certainly arrived when the sick begin to be in danger of death from sickness, infirmities, or simply age.

❑ The fruits of this anointing include comfort, peace, and courage in the face of death; union of the sick with the healing passion of Christ; pardon for sins, if the sick person cannot receive the Sacrament of Penance; and restoration to health, if this would be conducive to the soul's salvation.

Endnotes to Chapter Seven

1. Cf. Council of Trent, Session 14, November 25, 1551, *Doctrine on the Sacrament of Extreme Unction*, ch. 1 (DS 1695).

2. Council of Trent, Session 14, November 25, 1551, *Doctrine of the Sacrament of Extreme Unction*, ch. 1 (DS 1695).

3. Congregation for Divine Worship, *Rite of Anointing and Pastoral Care of the Sick*, published by authority of Pope Paul VI (December 7, 1972), Introduction, n. 8 (EV 4.1867).

4. Cf. *Rite of Anointing*, Introduction, n. 8 (EV 4.1867).

5. *Rite of Anointing*, Introduction, n. 9 (EV 4.1868).

6. *Rite of Anointing*, Introduction, n. 10 (EV 4.1869).

7. On the paragraph, cf. *Rite of Anointing*, Introduction, nn. 11-15 (EV 4.1870-1875).

8. *Rite of Anointing*, n. 76.

9. Pope Paul VI, Apostolic Constitution, *Sacram Unctionem Infirmorum* (November 30, 1972) (EV 4.1838-1848). Cf. Council of Trent, Session 14, November 25, 1551 *Doctrine on the Sacrament of Extreme Unction*, ch. 2 (DS 1696).

10. Cf. *Rite of Anointing*, n. 65.

11. *Rite of Anointing*, n. 5.

12. *Rite of Anointing*, n. 6.

13. *Rite of Anointing*, n. 7.

14. *Rite of Anointing*, n. 26.

15. St. Simeon of Thessalonica, *De Ordine Sepulturae* 336 (MG 155.686).

CHAPTER EIGHT

Christian Marriage:
Christ and Human Love

(*CCC* 1601-1658)

WE HAVE FOUND THAT the sacramental signs whereby Jesus has chosen to act on us through His Church, for the most part, make use of material elements — water, bread, wine, and oil. Marriage has a more sublime sign, one taken from human love. The sacramental sign is expressed in a pledge of enduring commitment. The love of husband and wife for each other signifies God's eternal love for His people and the love that binds Christ and His Church together.

The Church honors the married vocation and recognizes the supreme compliment Christ has paid to marriage in giving it sacramental status. The Church proclaims marriage a sacred sign, a sacrament, an act of worship, a reminder of Christ's love, an effective means by which He acts to make human love capable of being lasting, faithful, and fruitful, like His own love of the Church.

In this chapter we discuss covenant love in marriage, the relation of virginity and marriage, and the threefold good of marriage: offspring, fidelity, and the sacrament. Also treated here are the problem of broken marriages, the actions taken by the Church to guard the married state, and the vocation of married persons to holiness.

Covenant Love in Marriage

In the Old Testament, marriage was not sacred in our sense, nor was it celebrated with a religious ceremony. Yet marriage was preordained by God, who established it at the climax of creation. As the *Catechism of the Catholic Church* teaches:

> Sacred Scripture begins with the creation of man and woman in the image and likeness of God and concludes with a vision of

the wedding-feast of the Lamb. Scripture speaks throughout of marriage and its "mystery," its institution and the meaning God has given it, its origin and its end, its various realizations throughout the history of salvation, the difficulties arising from sin and its renewal "in the Lord" in the New Covenant of Christ and the Church.

— *CCC* 1602

As there are two accounts of creation, so there are two accounts of the institution of marriage. Each indicates an element of the meaning of marriage, and both themes are joined throughout the history of marriage down to the present. In the first creation account, procreation is stressed:

So God created man in His own image, in the image of God He created him; male and female He created them. And God blessed them, and God said to them, "Be fruitful and multiply, and fill the earth and subdue it."

— Gen 1:27-28

In the other account, the companionship of man and woman comes to the fore. All the animals were created, "but for the man there was not found a helper fit for him." But after the woman was created, the man said: "This at last is bone of my bones and flesh of my flesh." The sacred writer adds: "Therefore a man leaves his father and his mother and cleaves to his wife, and they become one flesh" (Gen 2:20-24).

God's ancient design of faithful monogamy was not preserved — because of "your hardness of heart," as Jesus was to say to the Pharisees (Mt 19:8).

Nevertheless, exclusive attachment was prized in the Old Testament. While the wife was subject to her husband, she was no mere chattel, as with the pagans. The famous portrait of the ideal wife in the Book of Proverbs shows her as a partner with responsibilities and dignity (cf. Prov 31:10-31). The Song of Songs reveals a passionate dialogue between two free partners whose love is obviously undivided. It thus presents a picture of marriage as a union of love in ancient Israel. The history of Tobit shows a deeply religious home from which his son Tobias goes to marry Sarah and enter with her into a union at once truly loving and pleasing to the Lord.

The New Covenant

Both the Song of Songs and Tobit introduce us into Jewish households after the exile. At this time, too, the sages who wrote the Wisdom literature were praising monogamy and urging fidelity in marriage (cf. Prov 5:1-23; 6:20-35). Malachi wrote:

> "So take heed to yourselves, and let none be faithless to the wife of his youth. For I hate divorce, says the LORD the God of Israel."
>
> — Mal 2:15-16

He here also speaks of marriage as a covenant **between a man and a woman**, comparing it to the covenant of God with Israel.

The climax of this long saga of love covenant and marriage, and the point at which marriage becomes a sacrament in the New Covenant, is noted in St. Paul's epistle to the Ephesians:

> Husbands, love your wives, as Christ loved the church and gave Himself up for her, that He might sanctify her, having cleansed her by the washing of water with the word, that He might present the church to Himself in splendor, without spot or wrinkle or any such thing, that she might be holy and without blemish. Even so husbands should love their wives as they do their own bodies. He who loves his wife loves himself. For no man ever hates his own flesh, but nourishes and cherishes it, as Christ does the church, because we are members of His body. "For this reason a man shall leave his father and mother and be joined to his wife, and the two shall become one." This is a great mystery, and I take it to mean Christ and the church.
>
> — Eph 5:25-32

Perhaps we can best understand what the apostle is saying here by starting at the end. The word translated as "mystery" is *sacramentum* in Latin and *mysterion* in Greek. It is the very word St.

Paul uses and enlarges on at the beginning of his letter, in describing the hidden plan of God whereby all are to be united in Christ: the mystery of God in Christ, the Paschal Mystery, which is at the center and heart of the New Covenant. What the apostle says about marriage, therefore, is related to or falls within this divine plan. The union of Christ with His Church is so intimate as to find no more apt comparison than the relation of husband and wife. Furthermore, since the union of Christ with His Church is sanctifying, making her holy, so the union of husband and wife is mutually sanctifying because it is situated within the mystery of Christ's union with His Church. This is especially so since Christ "gave Himself up" for the Church, purifying her. In this way, the union of husband and wife is drawn into Christ's sacrificial love for His Church, and thus into the mystery of His death and resurrection.

Marriage, then, is a sacrament between the baptized. It is a covenant between a man and a woman, committing them to live with each other in a bond of married love whose charter was established by God. This covenant is a symbol of the undying covenant love established by Christ with His Church in the Paschal Mystery. It is an encounter with Christ which makes effective the graces it signifies, the graces needed to make human love enduring, faithful, and fruitful, and so a suitable image of the love between Christ and His Church.

Marriage as the Union of a Man and Woman

Jesus taught the original meaning of the union of man and woman as willed by the Creator from the beginning. In His preaching He reminded His listeners that God Himself willed marriage as the union of one man and one woman. Marriage is the union of a man and woman, and is to be defined as such. In recent times in the face of societal challenges to the definition of marriage, the Church continues to teach with love and with clarity that marriage is the union of a man and woman who freely express their consent.

Scripture affirms that man and woman were created for one another. The *Catechism of the Catholic Church* teaches, "The vocation to marriage is written in the very nature of man and woman as they come from the hand of the Creator." The *Catechism* also reminds us:

> Marriage is not a purely human institution... the well being of the individual person and of both human and Christian society is closely bound up with the healthy state of conjugal and family life.
>
> — *CCC* 1603

From Sacred Scripture and Tradition, the Church confidently asserts, "Marriage belongs by nature to the relationship between a man and a woman."

Throughout time and across cultures, marriage has had a specific meaning: it is the union of a man and woman open to creating and nurturing children, with their unique and complementary gifts. This union of one man and woman is integral to the key purpose of marriage: the good of the spouses, and the openness to creating and raising children. By definition, marriage must be between a man and a woman.

Marriage, raised to the dignity of a sacrament in the union of one man and one woman, imitates Christ's love for the Church. This covenant of love between a man and a woman gives children a stable context, the home, in which they are created and nurtured, benefiting from the unique gifts of both father and mother. Marriage protects the rights of children to have — and benefit from — both a father and a mother. Marriage defined as the union of a man and a woman fosters the good of society through the good of the family as the "domestic church," a community of grace and prayer, and a school of human virtues and of Christian charity (*CCC* 1666).

Marriage and Virginity

Although St. Paul is a striking witness to the sanctity of marriage, he also commends warmly another way of life, that of virginity or celibacy.

> I want you to be free from anxieties. The unmarried man is anxious about the affairs of the Lord, how to please the Lord;

but the married man is anxious about worldly affairs, how to
please his wife, and his interests are divided. And the unmar-
ried woman or girl is anxious about the affairs of the Lord,
how to be holy in body and spirit; but the married woman is
anxious about worldly affairs, how to please her husband.

— 1 Cor 7:32-34

We have here indicated an alternate form of Christian life.
The same faith that honors marriage honors also that form of life
that forgoes the blessings of marriage precisely to further God's
kingdom and to bear a striking witness to faith in eternal life. A
life of Christian virginity may be lived in a religious community
or in the midst of secular responsibilities. For those called to such
a life, virginity offers a richer freedom to give themselves more
exclusively to the Lord. Virginity is a forceful way of expressing
faith in eternal life while "the form of this world is passing away"
(1 Cor 7:31).

We can understand the apparent paradox of the teaching that
describes marriage as a sacrament, and yet recommends virginity,
if we see both these ways as ultimately leading to God's love. In
the context of that love, the apostolic recommendations are not
contradictory — and even the paradox disappears.

Those joined in sacramental marriage are a visible sign of
God's love for the Church and of God's love for mankind. They
remind us all of God's love, and of the fact that all love comes
from God, for "God is love" (1 Jn 4:16), and should lead back to
God. Celibates on their part, while renouncing marriage, do not
renounce love: they are rather witnesses in a special way to that
greater love of Christ, of which marriage itself is a sign. They are
reminders to all that married love, sacred as it is, is transitory as
a means to that perfect love of God and one another that we are
to strive for and to have perfected in eternal life. Both married
love and perfect chastity should direct the heart toward eternity
and love fulfilled. The sacramental meaning of marriage points
to this. So also does the life of those vowed to perfect chastity;
their generous love should "recall to the minds of all the faithful that wondrous marriage decreed by God which is to be fully

revealed in the future age in which the Church has Christ as its only Spouse" (*PC* 12). The married and celibate vocations, then, far from being opposed to each other, support each other within the basic Christian vocation to seek holiness in love.

The Threefold Good of Marriage

"In marriage, let the goods of marriage be loved: offspring, fidelity, and the sacrament."[1] In these few words St. Augustine crystallized the teaching of faith on the purposes of matrimony, the goods for which God established and sanctified it. He takes the two goods of marriage already indicated in the creation accounts in Genesis, offspring and fidelity, and crowns them with the New Testament creation of sacrament. In so doing he provides a framework for the study of Christian marriage, a framework that has been used by the Church to this day (cf. *GS* 48).

Conjugal Love

"The first natural tie of human society," says St. Augustine, "is man and wife."[2] The Second Vatican Council calls marriage "a community of love" (*GS* 47). Mutual fidelity, at its minimum and considered negatively, forbids intercourse with anyone other than one's married partner; thus it is a bulwark to protect conjugal love.

> The intimate partnership of married life and love has been established by the Creator and qualified by His laws and is rooted in the conjugal covenant of irrevocable personal consent.... As a mutual gift of two persons, this intimate union and the good of the children impose total fidelity on the spouses and argue for an unbreakable oneness between them.
>
> — *GS* 48

Mutual and loving fidelity presupposes the fundamental equality of the partners in marriage:

> Firmly established in the Lord, the unity of marriage will radiate from the equal personal dignity of wife and husband, a dignity acknowledged by equal and total love.
>
> — *GS* 48

Nor can this equality be taken for granted even today. One of the Church's first tasks, in order to make Christian marriage possible, was to secure this basic personal equality. The words of Jesus recorded in the Gospel laid the foundation for this by teaching what was then a revolutionary idea, namely, that the mutual duties of husband and wife are the same:

> "Whoever divorces his wife and marries another, commits adultery against her, and if she divorces her husband and marries another, she commits adultery."
>
> — Mk 10:11-12

St. Paul carried this principle of equal rights into the home:

> For the wife does not rule over her own body, but the husband does; likewise the husband does not rule over his own body, but the wife does. Do not refuse one another except perhaps by agreement for a season, that you may devote yourselves to prayer.
>
> — 1 Cor 7:4-5

The Fathers and theologians, and the Second Vatican Council, sometimes speak of conjugal love as friendship. "Friendship" may seem to some a weak word for so close a union; but "friendship" is, in fact, a rich concept. Friendship is the most perfect form of love: Christ calls those bound most intensely to Him by divine love His friends (cf. Jn 15:15). For friendship, in its most authentic form, is an unselfish and mutual love persons have for each other, as each knows he or she is loved by the other. In sincere friendship, the tie of love is enduring, for it is not based on the hope of gratification from personal traits that can fade with time, but on the free and firm commitment of each to pursue the good of the other, for the other's sake.[3] To speak of married friendship is to recognize the fundamental equality of the husband and wife, and, therefore, the possibility of intimate sharing of life not only on the physical level but also on the level of mind and spirit. Such married friendship must be the human component of Christian conjugal love, which is authentic human love made fruitful by divine grace, and thereby transformed into an expression of charity. Unlike mere eroticism, it does not exploit the sensate, nor, on the other hand, does it strain for an impossible angelism; it seeks to integrate sexuality into the "new nature created after the likeness of God in true righteousness and holiness" (Eph 4:24).

Christian conjugal love "therefore far excels erotic inclination, which, selfishly pursued, soon enough fades wretchedly away" (*GS* 49). Yet:

> [This love] is eminently human since it is directed from one person to another through an affection of the will; it involves the good of the whole person, and can therefore enrich the expressions of body and mind with unique dignity, ennobling these expressions as special ingredients and signs of the friendship distinctive of marriage. This love the Lord has deigned to heal, perfect, and exalt with a special gift of grace and charity.
>
> — *GS* 49

With this special gift, a divine element has introduced into the human relationship between the spouses, assimilating it to the love of God and giving it the durability and power of this love:

> Christian couples, therefore, nourish and develop their marriage by undivided affection, which wells up from the fountain of divine love, while in a merging of human and divine love, they remain faithful in body and mind, in good times as in bad.[4]

Offspring

It may seem a belaboring of the obvious to mention offspring, children, as a blessing and purpose of marriage. Yet this could not be taken for granted in St. Augustine's time, nor can it now in our own. In that earlier age, the Manichaeans attacked marriage itself as evil — and hence, the offspring of marriage as well. In the world today there is no Manichaeanism as such, but there is a widespread attitude hostile to the procreative good and intent on weakening the bond between marriage and concern for new life.

The Second Vatican Council has reaffirmed in our time that the procreation of children is a basic good of marriage, defined as the union of a man and woman. This good cannot be assailed without harming conjugal love. The distinctive traits of marriage are ordered to the good of offspring. Married love must be faithful and enduring precisely to unite husband and wife in a love of such strength and personal concern that they can suitably carry out the duties of parents:

> Marriage and conjugal love are by their nature ordained toward the begetting and educating of children. Children are really the supreme gift of marriage.
>
> — GS 50[5]

This in no way detracts from the other purposes of marriage:

> Hence, while not making the other purposes of matrimony of less account, the true practice of conjugal love, and the whole meaning of family life which results from it, have this aim: that the couple be ready with stout hearts to cooperate with the love of the Creator and the Savior who through them will enlarge and enrich his own family day by day.
>
> — GS 50

This does not mean that parents should bring children into the world irresponsibly. As we have noted in an earlier chapter, Christian couples may indeed rightly reflect on the number of children they can wisely bring into this world, taking into account here all relevant factors. At the same time, however, they will rule out any and all forms of artificial birth control.

"God is love" (1 Jn 4:8). Because He is love, He has created us. There could be no other motive for this except to extend, diffuse, and share His boundless goodness. His love is so vast, so limitless, that He pours it forth into creation. It is to be expected, then, that in willing to share His love with men, He would also will to share with them the creative power of His love. This He does in making them capable of conjugal love, which is procreative:

> Parents should regard as their proper mission the task of transmitting human life and educating those to whom it has been transmitted. They should realize that they are coopera-

tors with the love of God the Creator, and are, so to speak, the interpreters of that love.

— GS 50

Their mutual love also bursts its bounds into creativity. For this, all the living can be grateful.

The Sacrament

The third good, or blessing, of marriage is sacramentality. Marriage is a covenant of indissoluble love. It is a sacred sign recalling and drawing upon the perpetual love between Christ and His Church. Like that covenant, a consummated sacramental marriage is entirely indissoluble. It endures until death.

The ministers of the sacrament of matrimony are the matrimonial partners themselves. The priest assisting at a marriage "must ask for and obtain the consent of the contracting parties" (*SC* 77). The consummation of the marriage seals it in a personal and mutual self-surrender of sexual union:

> But the grace which would perfect the natural love and confirm the indissoluble unity, and sanctify the persons married, Christ Himself, the instructor and perfecter of the venerable sacraments, merited for us by His passion.[6]

Marriage in the sense of covenanted love — sacred, solemn, serious — of itself requires indissoluble union after the model of God's love.

> The intimate partnership of married life and love has been established by the Creator and qualified by His laws, and is rooted in the conjugal covenant of irrevocable personal consent.

— GS 48

Marriage arises in the covenant of marriage, or irrevocable consent, which each partner freely bestows on and accepts from the other. This intimate union and the good of the children impose total fidelity on each of them and argue for an unbreakable oneness between them. Christ the Lord raised this union to the dignity of a sacrament so that it might more clearly recall and more easily reflect His own unbreakable union with His Church.[7]

Here, marriage is seen as a lifelong companionship, reflecting Christ's self-sacrificing and redeeming love in His new covenant with the Church (cf. *GS* 48).

The Church teaches that marriage, even as a natural institution, cannot be dissolved by the will of the partners or by any human authority.[8] To teach this is certainly not to teach that it is easy to remain faithful until death in marriage, or to say that married partners can succeed in doing so without the grace of God. But the Church does teach that by divine law, marriage demands such faithfulness, and that only special divine authority can legitimately dissolve such a bond. "So they are no longer two but one. What therefore God has joined together let no man put asunder" (Mt 19:6).

In some cases God does permit the dissolution of a purely natural bond of marriage — that is, one not contracted by two baptized persons. In the case of married unbelievers, one of whom becomes a Christian, the Church may permit the Christian to remarry, if the unbelieving spouse refuses to live peacefully with him or her. The Church has so understood the words of St. Paul (cf. 1 Cor 7:12-16), and has judged that in such cases God gives it the right to dissolve a nonsacramental marriage. This right is called the Pauline privilege. The Church, starting from this principle and recalling the "power of the keys" given to it, continues where conditions warrant to dissolve the natural, nonsacramental marriage in favor of the Faith.

But the Church has firmly proclaimed and always taught that a sacramental marriage between Christians in which there has been true matrimonial consent and consummation is absolutely indissoluble except by death of one of the partners. A sacrament recalling Christ's undying love for the Church, it is expressed in a binding tie that endures for life, no matter what happens between the spouses.[9]

Special Marriage Questions

In no area of life with all its problems do people suffer grief and anxiety more than in broken marriages. Catholics are not exempt from the pressures that make for such difficulties; the number of those divorced, and perhaps remarried, outside the Church presents us with an urgent pastoral concern.

The Church, faithful to the word of Christ that excludes divorce (cf. Mt 19:3-12; Mk 10:1-12), does not and cannot permit divorce and remarriage as a solution to these problems.[10] Such a solution, while it might seem kind to individuals in painful situations, is excluded by the divine command. Moreover, the good of husbands, wives, and children generally is that the enduring force of the marriage covenant be affirmed. Precisely because it is not dissoluble, married couples are assisted in their efforts to overcome the grave obstacles that can threaten any married life.

Still the Church does, when there are grave reasons for this, permit the separation of married partners from common life together.[11]

In some extreme circumstances, it can be imprudent for a couple to try to continue to live together. Such cases, however, never justify any claim to a right to dissolve the sacramental marriage bond, or a right to enter on a new marriage.

Some apparent marriages that "fail" were, in fact, never true marriages. No real marriage covenant was established if one or both of the partners failed to give, or was incapable of giving, free consent; or if one or both did not intend a real marriage, a bond of faithful love at least in principle open to offspring. If for any reason an apparent marriage was not a genuine marriage from the start, it may be possible to obtain from the Church an official acknowledgment of that fact, that is, an annulment, or, more exactly, a decree of nullity. Each diocese is required to have a matrimonial tribunal or court to hear and judge matrimonial cases. Should it be determined that one had not been validly married, genuine marriage with another partner would not be excluded.

Since Christ forbids divorce, the Church wishes to guard carefully entrance into the married state. Normally Catholics can be married validly only in the presence of a priest and witnesses.[12] The priest assisting at a marriage, who is to be the bishop or pastor of the place or his delegate, has the responsibility to see that the couple is in fact free to marry, that they receive sufficient instruction to realize the importance and dignity of the sacrament they are to receive, and that they are aware of the purposes and meaning of marriage and are entering into a genuine marriage covenant.

Impediments

To guard the married state, the Church has also the right to proclaim the existence of, and to establish, impediments to marriage. An impediment is a circumstance which, because of divine or ecclesiastical law, causes a marriage to be invalid.

The Church teaches, for example, that impotence, when it precedes the marriage and is permanent, makes a marriage invalid by the very law of nature, and that the same natural law excludes the possibility of a valid marriage between certain very close relatives.[13] Other impediments include lack of sufficient age, a preexisting and existing marriage, prior reception of Holy Orders, prior assumption of a solemn vow of chastity in a religious institute, and certain prior crimes.[14] The attempted marriage of a Catholic with an unbaptized person without a prior dispensation is also declared invalid.

Church law also declares marriage to be illicit in certain cases. For example, it forbids marriage between a Catholic and a baptized non-Catholic. Should a Catholic wish to marry a baptized non-Catholic, permission for such a marriage must first be obtained from the bishop. The bishop can grant permission for such a marriage if there is a reasonable cause. Before granting permission, the Church seeks to see to it that the threats to a successful marriage that often arise from differences in faith are countered by taking steps to guard the faith of the Catholic partner for which the Church has special responsibility, and to provide for the proper instruction to assist each of the partners.[15]

Invalid Marriages

A Catholic who is knowingly a partner in an invalid marriage is in reality and before God not married to his or her apparent spouse. Hence performance of the marriage act within that union is not a sacred and holy seal of married love, but really a wrongful use of sex. Those who have seriously disobeyed divine or ecclesiastical law by entering into an invalid marriage, and have perhaps committed many sins within that union, have a duty to return to the state of grace as quickly as possible, and certainly to abstain from Holy Communion until they do so. Some solution is always possible, even in the most difficult cases. At times one must accept a considerable amount of self-denial and bear the cross generously; but God's grace is able to make even difficult burdens bearable. Even if individuals feel that they do not now have the moral strength to do what the law of God demands of them, they ought not despair. In prayer, in faithful attendance at Mass, in doing the works of Christian love, they can with God's grace gradually acquire the courage needed to do with peace whatever is necessary. Pastors and diocesan marriage tribunals will try to be of assistance to those in invalid marriages. Those seeking a good conscience in these matters must remember that their consciences are to be formed in the light of Church teaching. Every solution that is reached must be entirely faithful to the command of Christ that consummated and sacramental marriages can in no way be dissolved or treated as though they can be.[16]

The Married Vocation

Although indissolubility undergirds conjugal love, it does not exhaust the meaning of the marriage covenant. The Church "is believed to be holy in a way which cannot fail. For Christ... loved the Church as His bride, delivering Himself up for her, so that He might sanctify her (cf. Eph. 5:25-26) . . . Therefore, in the Church all... are called to holiness" (*LG* 39).

The Second Vatican Council spoke of how that principle embraces those who enter the sacramental covenant:

> Married couples and Christian parents should follow their own proper path to holiness by faithful love, sustaining one another in grace throughout the entire length of their lives. They should imbue their offspring, lovingly welcomed from God, with Christian truth and evangelical virtues. For thus can they offer all men an example of unwearying and generous love, build up the brotherhood of charity, and stand as the witnesses to and cooperators in the fruitfulness of Holy Mother

Church. By such lives, they signify and share in that very love with which Christ loved His Bride and because of which He delivered Himself up on her behalf.

— *LG* 41

Pope Pius XI had stated this teaching for the married:

This outward expression of love in family life not only embraces mutual help, but should also extend to this, and indeed should have this as its primary purpose, that the married partners help each other in forming and perfecting themselves daily more fully in the interior life, so that through their partnership in life they may advance ever more and more in virtue, and especially that they may grow in true love towards God and their neighbors, on which indeed "depends the whole law and the prophets" (Mt 22:40). For all men, of every condition, in whatever honorable walk of life they may be, can and ought to imitate the most perfect example of holiness placed before man by God, namely, Christ our Lord, and by God's grace to arrive at the summit of perfection, as is proved by the example set us of many saints.[17]

Marriage and the Paschal Mystery

Christ's love for the Church is the pattern for married love. Christ's love was a sacrificial love, and it included suffering where necessary. "Greater love has no man than this, that a man lay down his life for his friends" (Jn 15:13). Such also is the love — for one another as well as for Himself — that He expects of His followers. "A new commandment I give to you, that you love one another; even as I have loved you, that you also love one another" (Jn 13:34). This is far more than loving one's neighbor as oneself; it goes beyond the Golden Rule, even to the limit: "By this we know love, that He laid down His life for us; and we ought to lay down our lives for the brethren" (1 Jn 3:16).

Now it is this sacrificial love that is the exemplar of Christian marriage and the sacrament, the mystery, the foreshadowing, through which Christ blesses the married couple. To love each other faithfully until death, they must learn to forgive each other and to bear crosses well. In raising a family, with all the joys and all the heartaches that implies, they will be required to give of self.

St. Paul exhorted: "Husbands, love your wives as Christ loved the church and gave Himself up for her..." (Eph 5:25). Thus the married couple is in a special way plunged into the mystery of the Lord's death and resurrection; through this sacrament, their love shares in the saving mystery of Christ and signifies its final perfection in the Church fully realized. This is why Christian marriage must be indissoluble, literally unto death. It is why the perfection of Christian love is so necessary to the married couple, lest human selfishness separate what God has joined together; and why, therefore, a special sacrament is given to foster such love. The marriage covenant must partake of the quality and durability of the love of Him who said: "I have loved you with an everlasting love" (Jer 31:3).

The celebration of marriage "normally should be within the Mass."[18] This also signifies its issuance from the Paschal Mystery. In the wedding Mass, the Liturgy of the Word "shows the importance of Christian marriage in the history of salvation and the duties and responsibilities of the couple in caring for the holiness of their children."[19]

Then in the Liturgy of the Eucharist, in which salvation history rises to its climax, the now-married couple enters the sacramental source of the Paschal Mystery and "eat this bread and drink the cup" to "proclaim the Lord's death until He comes" (1 Cor 11:26). Even in its ceremony, the Church seeks to enshrine and consecrate marriage by her most sublime possession, the mystery of the Faith.

Discussion Questions

1. Discuss the ways in which a couple entering into the Sacrament of Marriage reflect the Paschal Mystery of Christ's love for the Church.

2. Discuss the Church's teaching on God as the author of marriage as the unique union of one man and one woman that is raised to the dignity of the Sacrament of Marriage.

3. How can your family reflect more clearly its role as a "domestic church"? What kinds of support can you offer to couples in troubled marriages within your family, your parish, and society?

Additional References:

United States Catholic Catechism for Adults: Chapter 21 — "The Sacrament of Marriage."

Catechism of the Catholic Church, 1601-1658.

Pope Benedict XVI, *The Sacrament of Charity* (*Sacramentum Caritatis*). Post-Synodal Apostolic Exhortation, February 22, 2007.

Archdiocese of Washington, *Marriage Matters* (http://www.adw.org/family/marriage.asp).

Words to Remember...

❑ God is the author of marriage, and Christ raised marriage for His followers to the dignity of a sacrament.

❑ Marriage is the union of a man and woman open to creating and nurturing children, with their unique and complementary gifts.

❑ Through the Sacrament of Marriage, the spouses should grow in generous love of one another and rejoice in the goods for which marriage exists: faithful love, the joy of offspring, and the sacramental good — that is, the blessings of an enduring love like that between Christ and the Church.

❑ Christ taught that there is no human authority able to dissolve marriage.

❑ Those wishing to marry should prepare carefully for it; they should be certain they are free to marry.

❑ The ministers of the Sacrament of Matrimony are the matrimonial partners themselves; the bishop, priest, or deacon assisting at a marriage serves as a witness to the sacrament that the spouses confer on each other.

❑ An annulment does not dissolve a marriage; it is simply a declaration that an apparent marriage was never a true marriage, because of some serious flaw that it suffered from the beginning.

Endnotes to Chapter Eight

1. St. Augustine, *De Nuptiis et Concupiscientia* 1.17.19 (ML 44.424).
2. St. Augustine, *De Bono Coniugali* 1 (ML 40.373).
3. Cf. St. Thomas Aquinas, *Commentarium in Librum III Sententiarum*, q. 27, a. 2, c. See also Pope John Paul II, Apostolic Exhortation *Familiaris Consortio* (November 22, 1981), nn. 18-19 (EV 7.1582-1585).
4. Congregation of Rites, *Rite of Marriage*, published by authority of Pope Paul VI, March 19, 1969, Introduction, n. 3 (EV 3.867).
5. Cf. Pope John Paul II, Apostolic Exhortation *Familiaris Consortio* (November 22, 1981), nn. 36-41 (EV 7.1638-1661).
6. Council of Trent, Session 24, November 11, 1563, *Doctrine on the Sacrament of Matrimony* (DS 1799).
7. *Rite of Marriage*, Introduction, n. 2 (EV 3.866).
8. Cf. Council of Trent, Session 24, November 11, 1563, *Doctrine on the Sacrament of Matrimony* (DS 1797-1799, 1807); Pope Pius XI, Encyclical *Casti Connubii* (December 31, 1930) (DS 3712, 3724); Pope John Paul II, Apostolic Exhortation *Familiaris Consortio* (November 22, 1981), n. 20 (EV 7.1586-1588). Cf. also *GS* 48-49; AA 11.
9. See note 8.
10. Cf. Council of Trent, Session 24, November 11, 1563, *Doctrine on the Sacrament of Matrimony*, especially canons 7 and 8 (DS 1807, 1808). Proper pastoral treatment for disordered marriage is discussed in Pope John Paul II, Apostolic Exhortation *Familiaris Consortio* (November 22, 1981), nn. 77-85 (EV 7.1768-1804).
11. Cf. *Code of Canon Law*, canons 1152-1153; Council of Trent, Session 24, November 11, 1563, *Doctrine on the Sacrament of Matrimony*, canon 8 (DS 1808).
12. Cf. *Code of Canon Law*, canon 1108.1.
13. Cf. *Code of Canon Law*, canons 1084 and 1091.
14. Cf. *Code of Canon Law*, canons 1083, 1085, 1087, 1088, 1089, and 1090.
15. Cf. *Code of Canon Law*, canons 1124, 1125.
16. Cf. Pope John Paul II, Apostolic Exhortation *Familiaris Consortio* (November 22, 1981), n. 84 (EV 7.1796-1802). Cf. also Congregation for the Doctrine of the Faith, Letter to all the bishops (April 11, 1973) (EV 4.2383).
17. Pope Pius XI, Encyclical *Casti Connubii* (December 31, 1930) (cf. DS 3707).
18. *Rite of Marriage*, Introduction, n. 6 (EV 3.870).
19. *Rite of Marriage*, Introduction, n. 6 (EV 3.870).

Conclusion

To be human is to have aspirations and desires. At root, the deepest human desire is for God. For we are made by God, for union with God and communion with one another. The sacraments of the Church are offered to us as unique means to deeper union with Christ, within the communion of the Church.

The Sacraments: A Continuing Encounter with Christ is an opportunity to grow in understanding of the sacramental life of the Catholic Church. However, study, discussion, and prayerful reflection are just the beginning. The sacramental catechesis offered in these pages is also an invitation to participate in and live personally the saving meaning of Jesus' Paschal Mystery, the heart of every sacramental celebration. Reflection becomes truly effective and life-changing when it leads to a renewed encounter with Christ's continuing presence among us, in His Word and in the sacraments of the Church.

To partake of the riches of the Church's sacramental life is to be personally conformed to the Lord Jesus in and through His sacramental presence. Adult faith formation yields rich fruit when daily life is gradually renewed and transformed through participation in the holy mysteries celebrated in the sacraments. Study, discussion, reflection, prayer, and daily conversion flow one from the other. For as Pope Benedict XVI notes:

> The aim of all Christian education is to train the believer in an adult faith that can make him a "new creation," capable of bearing witness in His surroundings to Christian hope.
> — *Sacramentum Caritatis*, 64

Through the ministry of the Church, we receive the sacraments of God's strengthening, forgiving, and healing love. The sacraments mark important moments of life: birth, vocation, sickness, and death. And they correspond to our deepest human desires: to belong, to forgive and to be forgiven, to be healed, and to live fully one's vocation in life.

The Church offers the sacraments as gifts of divine grace for the daily journey of faith and life. To these gifts of Christ's continuing presence our human response is faith and gratitude, expressed in Christian discipleship and witness. As Pope Benedict XVI reminded us of the gift of the Church's sacramental life when he offered these challenging words during his pastoral visit to the United States:

> Through the surpassing power of Christ's grace, entrusted to frail human ministers, the Church is constantly reborn and each of us is given the hope of a new beginning. Let us trust in the Spirit's power to inspire conversion, to heal every wound, to overcome every division, and to inspire new life and freedom. How much we need these gifts!
> — Homily, Washington Nationals Stadium, April 17, 2008